MW01593765

Mind Over Matter.

Punum Bhatia

Mind Over Matter:

Contributing Factors to Self-Efficacy in Montessori Teachers

LAP LAMBERT Academic Publishing

Impressum / Imprint

Bibliografische Information der Deutschen Nationalbibliothek: Die Deutsche Nationalbibliothek verzeichnet diese Publikation in der Deutschen Nationalbibliografie; detaillierte bibliografische Daten sind im Internet über http://dnb.d-nb.de abrufbar.
Alle in diesem Buch genannten Marken und Produktnamen unterliegen warenzeichen-, marken- oder patentrechtlichem Schutz bzw. sind Warenzeichen oder eingetragene Warenzeichen der jeweiligen Inhaber. Die Wiedergabe von Marken, Produktnamen, Gebrauchsnamen, Handelsnamen, Warenbezeichnungen u.s.w. in diesem Werk berechtigt auch ohne besondere Kennzeichnung nicht zu der Annahme, dass solche Namen im Sinne der Warenzeichen- und Markenschutzgesetzgebung als frei zu betrachten wären und daher von jedermann benutzt werden dürften.

Bibliographic information published by the Deutsche Nationalbibliothek: The Deutsche Nationalbibliothek lists this publication in the Deutsche Nationalbibliografie; detailed bibliographic data are available in the Internet at http://dnb.d-nb.de.
Any brand names and product names mentioned in this book are subject to trademark, brand or patent protection and are trademarks or registered trademarks of their respective holders. The use of brand names, product names, common names, trade names, product descriptions etc. even without a particular marking in this work is in no way to be construed to mean that such names may be regarded as unrestricted in respect of trademark and brand protection legislation and could thus be used by anyone.

Coverbild / Cover image: www.ingimage.com

Verlag / Publisher:
LAP LAMBERT Academic Publishing
ist ein Imprint der / is a trademark of
OmniScriptum GmbH & Co. KG
Heinrich-Böcking-Str. 6-8, 66121 Saarbrücken, Deutschland / Germany
Email: info@lap-publishing.com

Herstellung: siehe letzte Seite /
Printed at: see last page
ISBN: 978-3-659-64863-2

Zugl. / Approved by: Denver, University of Colorado Denver, Diss., 2012

ABSTRACT

Interpreting Albert Bandura's term "self-efficacy" as the individual's belief in his own abilities to succeed in spite of the given circumstances, this study seeks to identify the influences which lead to self-efficacy in Montessori teachers. In order to evaluate perceptions of self-efficacy, 35 pre-service teachers in the United States were surveyed prior to beginning their Montessori teaching and again during the internship stage of their training. As Bandura asserted that self-efficacy stems from four possible sources: mastery experience; vicarious experience; verbal or social persuasion; and physiological state (1997), the same subjects were given an additional questionnaire to determine which factors most affected their efficacy. Multiple regression was then used to examine the relationship between those factors and the teachers' self-reported efficacy. Following this data collection, four teachers from the high self-efficacy group and four teachers from the low self-efficacy group were interviewed to reveal detailed qualitative information regarding the influences on their classroom efficacy. The research indicates that Montessori teachers with high levels of self-efficacy have strong mastery experiences that support their attitudes and desired professional goals. The quantitative results also show that an emotional state associated with past experiences is the second best contributor to self-efficacy. Considering that self-efficacy may be most malleable during the early stages of learning, the results of this study serve to enhance the teacher-training experience though the analysis of early obstacles.

The form and content of this abstract are approved. I recommend its publication.

Approved: Alan Davis

DEDICATION

In honor of teachers, who awaken children's curiosity and instill a lifelong

love of learning.

ACKNOWLEDGEMENTS

I am very grateful to many people who have supported me throughout the process of completing my doctoral program and dissertation. This project would not have been possible without the help and support of my dissertation committee. Thank you Dr. Alan Davis for sugarcoating my bombardment of questions by telling me I was simply "doing my duty" and to the rest of my committee members, Dr. Donna Wittmer, Dr. Joanna Dunlap and Dr. Ellen Hall for taking my vague ideas and shaping them into a coherent paper. Dr. William Goodwin, your wisdom, dedication to learning and wit are sorely missed. Special thanks also go out to my parents and my children, who did not let me give up and who regaled me with their own tales of all-nighters. Finally, I would like to acknowledge the Montessori community—from Calcutta to Colorado—who has continuously inspired me for the past thirty years.

PHOTOGRAPHS

I wish to acknowledge the following organization for the photographs used in this document: Montessori Casa International, Denver CO. for the photographs used in Figures 1, 2 and 3.

TABLE OF CONTENTS

CHAPTER

LIST OF FIGURES

FIGURE

LIST OF TABLES

TABLE

STYLE NOTE

This thesis includes quotations in which the pronouns 'he' or 'it' are used as a generic reference to 'the child'. This represents the direct translations of grammatical gender as used in a language other than English.

In order to avoid wordiness, the teacher has been referred to as 'she' throughout this text. This is by no means intended to be a discriminatory decision, but merely reflects the demographics of teacher training programs.

CHAPTER 1

INTRODUCTION

Purpose of the Research

"The first thing required of a teacher is that he be rightly disposed for his task"
(Montessori, 1966, p.149*)*.

In light of the current educational reform movement, higher education programs are focusing on the professional dispositions of teacher candidates as they review their curriculum standards and agendas (Darling-Hammond & McLaughlin, 1995). Researchers, practitioners, and others with a vested interest in teacher education believe that information of subject matter and of pedagogical methods alone does not guarantee quality teachers or quality teaching—although these are necessary prerequisites for effective teacher preparation (Borko & Putnam, 1996; Pajares, 1992). Teachers are now finding it essential to reflect on teaching practices, as well as knowledge and pedagogy, to better meet the needs of their students (Darling-Hammond & McLaughlin, 1995). Dr. Albert Bandura, the social psychologist who devised the construct of self-efficacy, argued that successful performance depends not only on one's knowledge and skills but, more importantly, upon the individual's judgment in mobilizing that knowledge and skill set (1997). "Judgment," identified by Bandura as one's perceived self-efficacy, is a cognitive process that operates in all learning situations and acts as a mediator between learning and action.

As Albert Bandura assumed, "the task of creating learning environments conducive to development of cognitive competencies rests heavily on the talents and self-efficacy of teachers" (Bandura, 1997, p. 240). Perceived self-efficacy, as defined by Bandura, is the belief that an individual has the ability to carry out certain actions that result in a desired outcome (1997). A teacher's sense of efficacy is consistently recognized as an important attribute of effective teaching and has been positively correlated to teacher and student outcomes (Tschannen-Moran, Woolfolk Hoy, 1998). This theory is supported by research that shows "self-efficacy beliefs are strong predictors of behavior" (Woolfolk Hoy, 2004, p.4). How efficacious a person believes him or her to be influences the choice of activities, amount of effort spent, and the persistence put forth to complete the tasks when confronted with obstacles. Furthermore, teacher efficacy accounts for how competent a teacher feels in his ability to affect the performance of all students, no matter how unmotivated or difficult (Tschannen-Moran, Woolfolk Hoy, 1998). Much remains to be learned about self-efficacy, however, and how it develops in teachers. Unfortunately, simply identifying high and low-efficacy teachers will not provide information on increasing levels of efficacy. Instead, a deep understanding of the influences on teacher self-efficacy is needed. Schools of education and teacher preparation programs in particular need to be aware of the factors associated with increased levels of self-efficacy in order to produce the most capable, innovative, and dedicated teachers possible.

Montessori Pedagogy

Although the dispute continues in traditional teacher-education programs as to the relevance of dispositions in effective teaching practice, the concept is inherent to the Montessori teaching philosophy. Dr. Maria Montessori thought "the first step in the integral resolution of the problem of education must not, therefore, be taken toward the child, but toward the adult educator. He must change his moral attitudes. He must divest himself of many preconceptions" (1989, p. 20). Montessori's alternative approach to pedagogy promoted the natural ability of children to focus and to sustain their attention, a capacity that initiates a transition in the child's temperament from capricious and disorderly to self-disciplined (1989). Montessori viewed education as a means of putting the child in touch with the world around him/her and helping him/her to develop the skills s/he needs to embrace it. John Chattin-McNichols found that

> The Montessori program performs as well as most preschool programs in most areas, such as school readiness and intelligence... In the development of attentional strategies, general intelligence, achievement in academic areas, and especially in maintaining these gains, the Montessori Method performs better than most programs studied. (1992, p. 204)

The Montessori Method includes a personalized curriculum, close observations of children, and no reports cards among other innovations.

The 'Prepared Environment'

Considering the radical changes in our understanding and attitude towards cognitive development, it is startling to find that many of these insights were already

3

introduced by Dr. Maria Montessori. At the turn of the 20th century, Montessori

discovered a revolutionary way of directing young children's learning; in contrast to the

teacher-centered approach prevalent at the time, she realized that children learned more

effectively if adults provided them with a 'prepared environment' (See: Illustration 1)

that gave them a sense of equality and empowerment. In the calm, ordered space of the

Montessori 'prepared environment,' children work on activities of their own choosing

and at their own pace. They experience a blend of freedom and self-discipline in a place

specially designed to meet their developmental needs.

Figure 1.1: A 'prepared environment'

Montessori classrooms are "usually a large, open-feeling space, with low shelves, different sizes of tables that comfortably seat one to four children and chairs that are appropriately sized for the children in the classroom" (Lillard, 2005, p. 18). A collection of materials (apparatus) is displayed on the shelves, with everything carefully ordered and in its place (See: Illustration 2). The materials entice the child because they are placed in the centre of his/her vision, are within easy reach, and because they have a sensory appeal, varying in color, shape, size, texture, and possibilities of manipulation. The array of sensory contrasts, however, suggests purposeful variation rather than a random placement of brightly colored objects.

Figure 1.2: Carefully prepared shelf

The apparatus helps children learn basic concepts and relationships at different levels of abstraction by ensuring that the activities are based on physical manipulation of objects and progress through imagery to symbolic representation. The adults in the classroom unobtrusively demonstrate the use of the materials and then leave the child to work with them, intervening as needed. Children are absorbed in using these objects, selecting them from the shelves, taking them to a mat or small table, and working with them unrestrictedly before returning them to the shelf.

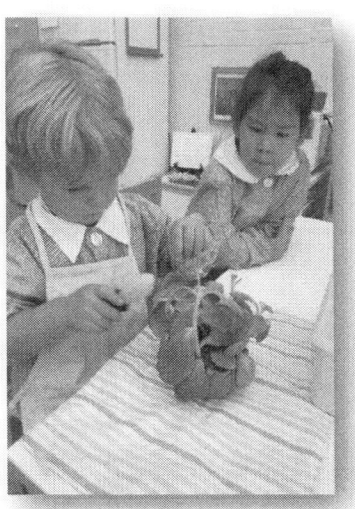 

Figure 1.3: Children concentrating on their work in a Montessori classroom

Montessori saw life in the classroom as interplay between the child, the environment, and the teacher. E. M. Standing calls the 'prepared environment' "the third factor in education" (1957, p.265). In traditional schools the teacher attempts to impart knowledge to the children through her resources and expects them to learn from her, usually in a group situation. Since the learning is undertaken mainly in the abstract and the amount of repetition is not under the students' control, such a system limits how much children learn and at what age the learning should occur. In the Montessori classroom though, this 'third factor' alters the dynamic between student and teacher. The child is free to act on his own impulses and to repeat activities until he has exhausted his interest. Instead of the power of the adult's persona controlling the child's natural flow, her energy is turned toward the environment. Standing illustrates this in the following diagram:

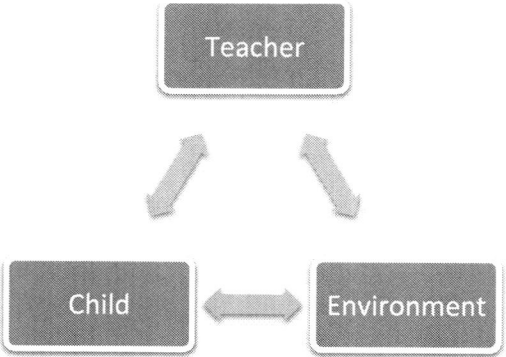

Figure 1.4: Flow of activity

The child learns mainly through the environment, while the teacher maintains the environment and supervises the children. In this way, each child learns independently and at his/her own pace. Standing describes the Montessori teacher as "a combination of a guardian angel with an information bureau" (1957, p.318). Thus, the Montessori teacher has a multi-faceted role, which means her initial training differs considerably from the standard teacher preparation.

The Prepared Adult

The Montessori teacher seeks to provide an atmosphere of productive calm as children move efficiently along in their learning, alternating between long periods of intense concentration and brief moments of recovery/reorganization (Oppenheimer, 1999). The teacher's goal is to help and to encourage the children, allowing them to develop self-reliance and inner discipline. Montessori believed that interrupting children when they were engaged in purposeful activity interferes with their momentum, interest, and inner workings of thought. "[The directress] understands and believes that the children must be free to choose their own occupations just as they must never be interrupted in their spontaneous activities"(2007, p. 240), wrote Montessori. Montessori placed the preparation of the teacher and the cultivation of her attitudes and values at the center of the process of becoming a teacher.

In Montessori teacher training, preparing the adult emotionally and spiritually is fundamental to the education of future teachers. According to Montessori,

The first essential is that the teacher should go through an inner, spiritual preparation; cultivate certain aptitudes in the moral order. This is the most difficult part of her training, without which all the rest is of no avail…She must study how to purify her heart and render it burning with charity towards the child. She must "put on humility," and above all, learn how to serve. She must learn how to appreciate and gather in all those tiny and delicate manifestations of the opening life in the child's soul. Ability to do this can only be attained through a genuine effort towards self-perfection. (Standing, 1957, p. 298)

Montessori was not the first advocate of pursuing self-knowledge. Carl Jung, the well-known psychoanalyst, advised, "if there is anything we wish to change in the child, we should first examine it and see whether it is not something that could better be changed in ourselves" (1940, p.285). J. G. Bennett echoed this advice writing, "whether we have to deal with children as parents or as teachers, our task begins with ourselves; and there is very much more to be derived by children from what those in contact with them do to put their own house in order than what they attempt to do to put the child's house in order" (1984, p. 82).

In her extensive writings, Montessori states that true preparation of the teaching adult comprises three levels of meticulous knowledge. The first two are technical familiarity with the materials (acquired through training) and scientific understanding of the true nature of the child through study and acute observation. The responsibility to uphold and to maintain this technical and scientific knowledge is absolutely essential. The third phase also requires understanding, but of the inner self for "the basis of this preparation consists in going through a fundamental change of outlook" (Standing, 1957, p. 298). Montessori identified this as a spiritual or moral preparation, which requires the recognition and removal of personal defenses built up over a lifetime. So "the training of

9

the teacher, who is to aid life, is something far more than a learning of ideas. It includes the training of character; it is a preparation of the spirit" (Montessori, 2007, p.120). What Montessori therefore asked of her teachers was that they no longer saw their role as that of simply one that imparts superior knowledge and understanding, but rather that of observer and catalyst between the children and the environment.

Montessori reasoned that teachers should have positive attitudes towards all children, regardless of the behavior they display when they first arrive at school. The teacher must have faith in the belief that the children will change for the better when they begin to concentrate on work and not label them on the basis of initial impressions. Montessori wrote, "We insist on the fact that a teacher must prepare himself interiorly by systematically studying himself so that he can tear out his most deeply rooted defects, those in fact which impede his relations with children" (1966, p. 149). The Montessori teacher undergoes a different type of training from the conventional teacher—even today when education generally shows signs of having absorbed many Montessori principles. Montessori considered an examination of her own personality as the teacher's starting point for training, reflecting on anger, impatience, favoritism, and other prejudices as a "spiritual preparation." Likewise, the teacher must foster the prepared environment; if she is too dominant in the classroom, she can actually be an obstacle to the children. Ideally, a teacher should regard herself as a sort of servant, ready to provide students with what they need without imposing herself on them.

The best preparation for teaching, according to Maria Montessori, is a study of one's self (2007); this can be very challenging for teachers who encounter Montessori for the first time. During the initial interview for a teacher training program, many candidates will gladly share their transcripts and discuss their academic successes or failures. On the subject of self -awareness and journal writing, however, few have undergone an in-depth study of their own values, beliefs, strengths, weaknesses, and habits. While some display excitement about this process, others show a lack of self-assurance and even discomfort at the idea. Montessori insisted,

> that a teacher must prepare himself interiorly by systematically studying himself so that he can tear out his most deeply rooted defects, those in fact which impede his relations with children. In order to discover these subconscious failings we have need of a special kind of instruction. We must see ourselves as another sees us. We must be willing to accept guidance if we wish to become effective teachers. (Montessori, 1966, p. 149)

As a result, the cohort of Montessori teachers usually falls into two categories: those who have mastered the materials, but who continue to struggle in the classroom; and those whose self-reflection encourage their confidence in responding to the children. These students come from different backgrounds and academic levels and it is possible that this impacts the way they teach.

Montessori teacher education is unique to others in placing more emphasis on developing self-awareness than on building theoretical knowledge. Inner preparation cannot be seen as effortless or resulting in an immediate transformation; it requires a lifetime of both deep reflection and passionate commitment. Given the inherent difficulty in changing existing beliefs, coupled with the relatively short duration of a teacher preparation program, developing a valid lens through which candidate self-efficacy can be examined is not a simple undertaking. Two separate studies, Henson (2002) and Tschannen-Moran and Woolfolk Hoy (1998), found that once efficacy beliefs are established they are harder to change. These studies indicate there is a small window of opportunity to establish and to potentially increase a teacher's self-efficacy; therefore, the time to affect change in a teacher's self-efficacy is early in the process of training and induction. The purpose of this study is to determine how best to incorporate efficacy-building components into teacher-training programs by gaining an understanding of the influences on self-efficacy for Montessori teachers. Considering the emphasis on persistent introspection and self-evaluation in Montessori training, it is evident that self-efficacy beliefs would also play a part in nurturing the Montessori teacher. Montessori noted that inner preparation "will give [the teacher] the balance and poise which he will need" (Montessori, 1966, p.153), which would naturally include the assessment of one's own abilities in the classroom. In this regard, it is somewhat surprising that the grooming of the Montessori teacher has not been studied in further depth.

Conceptual Framework

Despite the increasing interest in teacher self-efficacy over the years, no published research explores the interplay of sources and their influences on the development of Montessori teachers. Given that efficacy may be most malleable during the early stages of learning (Bandura, 1997), Woolfolk Hoy (2000) pointed out that self-efficacy of pre-service teachers is likely subject to change once they assume real teaching responsibilities.

12

Therefore, investigating pre-service teacher self-efficacy and how these beliefs are conceived and nurtured can provide significant information to professionals responsible for designing and implementing more meaningful teacher- preparation programs.

Self-efficacy means the judgment of one's ability to "produce desired results and forestall detrimental ones" through one's own actions (Bandura, 2001, p.10). Bandura added that "unless people believe they can produce desired effects by their actions, they have little incentive to act" (1997, p.3). This means a person who believes he is fully capable of completing a task will set appropriate goals, be wholly motivated, perceive his ability level as adequate to the task, and express interest in the outcome. Two people with the same skills and knowledge may undertake a task differently depending on their level of self-efficacy. This study is grounded in Bandura's social cognitive theory and, specifically, in his concept of self-efficacy.

Bandura (1997) proposes four sources of self-efficacy: mastery experiences; vicarious experiences; social persuasion; and physiological and affective states. Mastery experiences are the actual successful or unsuccessful outcomes of performing the task, which Bandura indicated is the most important determinant of self-efficacy as it provides authentic feedback regarding one's capabilities. It refers to the interpretations individuals make of their past performances. For instance, past successes create a strong sense of confidence for accomplishing similar future tasks, whereas failures can lower one's efficacy perceptions -- particularly if they occur in the early stages of learning. Bandura suggested that interpretations of past performance serve as a robust indicator of self-

13

efficacy and that failure was unlikely to affect it. A resilient sense of self-efficacy is when one has faced setbacks and overcome obstacles, as one can easily be discouraged by failure even after experiencing mild success. Therefore, the effects of failure on one's self-efficacy are partly dependent on the timing and the total pattern of experiences in which the failures occur. If the success is attributed to internal causes such as ability or effort, then self-efficacy is enhanced. However, if success is attributed to luck or the intervention of others, then self-efficacy may not be strengthened (Bandura, 1993; Pintrich & Schunk, 1996).

Bandura (1997) identified vicarious experiences as the second-most potent influence on self-efficacy. Vicarious experiences occur when a person sees someone with perceived similar ability perform the task or skill in question; this makes the observer feel that they too have the capabilities to succeed. On the other hand, observing someone fail in spite of large efforts lowers one's efficacy. The degree to which the observer identifies with the model therefore moderates the efficacy effect on the observer (Bandura, 1997). By observing and identifying oneself with efficacious models, the learner gathers information necessary to make judgments about his or her own capabilities. The more closely the observer identifies with the model, the stronger the impact on efficacy (Hoy, 2000).

Verbal or social persuasion, such as words of encouragement or moral support from others regarding one's performance, may also modify one's perceptions of efficacy. Such positive verbal messages or social persuasion could influence the individual to exert

14

extra effort, or to demonstrate the persistent behavior necessary to succeed when faced with difficult tasks. Alternatively, critical feedback could impede one's sense of self-efficacy. Bandura (1977, 1997) viewed verbal persuasion as a comparatively weak source of efficacy. Persuasion contributes to successful performances in the sense that a credible boost in self-efficacy leads a person to initiate the task, attempt new strategies, or try hard to succeed (Bandura, 1982). The potency of persuasion depends on the credibility, trustworthiness, and expertise of the persuader (Bandura, 1986).

The fourth informational source on self-efficacy is an individual's physiological or emotional state. High emotional arousal usually debilitates performance and results in the individual feeling extremely vulnerable to failure (Bandura 1977), so experiences of stress and anxiety may have a negative effect on the individual's beliefs about his capabilities. In a taxing situation, physical symptoms such as increased heart beat or sweaty palms can cause the individual to perceive ineptitude in performing a task. Typically, self-efficacy is raised in a positive emotional state and lowered in a negative emotional state (Bandura, 1997).

Using Bandura's theory of self-efficacy to evaluate Montessori pre-service teachers requires some modification and clarification (see Figure 2). In Montessori teacher training courses, mastery experience would include content knowledge based on Montessori philosophy, child development, observation and assessment, contemporary issues, health, safety and nutrition, as well as the six curriculum areas of the classroom. Students are expected to produce six albums with lesson plans on each of the curriculum

15

areas and to know the rationale and purpose behind each of the learning materials. Vicarious influence refers to the influence of others in the teaching field that the teacher-in-training could imitate; the internship mentor is particularly significant as the student teacher models classroom management style from him/her. Verbal or social persuasion denoted encouragement that the pre-service teacher receives from her/ his colleagues, teachers, and mentors. The final influence of emotional state illustrates the impact of stress and anxiety on efficacy beliefs. These four influences are then filtered through the individual's cognitive processing before becoming a measurable conduit/indicator of efficacy.

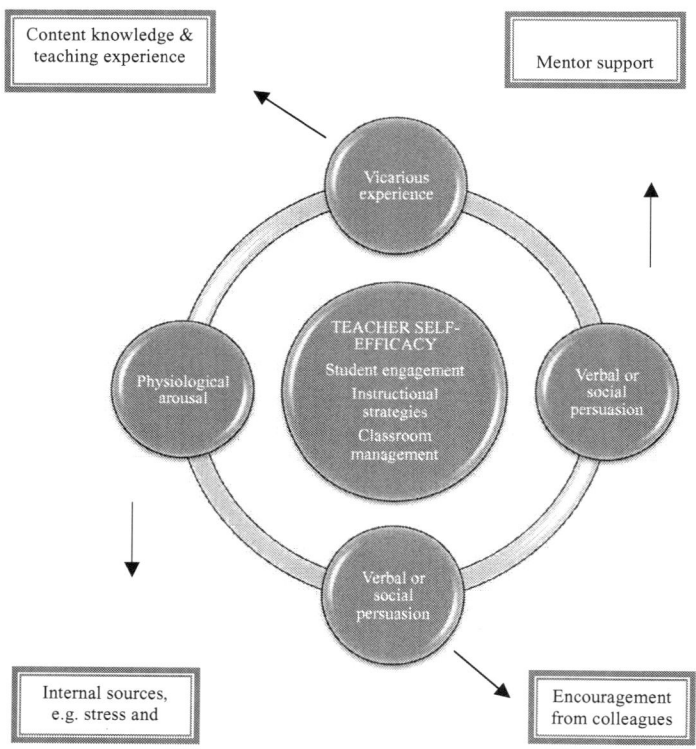

Figure 1.5: Conceptual framework of the study

Overview of the Study

One of the goals of this mixed methods research study is to determine how best to incorporate efficacy-building components into teacher-training programs by gaining an understanding of the influences on self-efficacy for Montessori teachers. The development of teacher- efficacy beliefs among prospective teachers has generated a great deal of research interest because once efficacy beliefs are established; they appear to be somewhat resistant to change (Hoy, 2000). Quantitatively, the study will examine the level of teacher self-efficacy and its influences. Each of these influences will be further explored through qualitative semi-structured interviews with the participants.

In this study, I will attempt to predict the influences on pre-service teacher self-efficacy; add to the current knowledge base; have a personal, social, and organizational impact upon the Montessori teaching profession; and gain a deeper understanding of the impact on teachers in general. The main objectives of this mixed methods inquiry are to (a) build a statistical model that significantly predicts the influences on Montessori pre-service teacher self-efficacy; (b) qualitatively examine the influences on Montessori teacher efficacy; and (c) gain a better understanding of the multiple influences on those students who exhibit high and low self- efficacy. Therefore, the following research questions are explored:

1. Do the independent variables of mastery experience, vicarious experience, verbal or social persuasion, and physiological arousal significantly predict self- efficacy among Montessori pre-service teachers?

2. How do Montessori pre-service teachers with high and low levels of self-efficacy explain the influences of mastery experience, vicarious experience, verbal or social persuasion, and physiological arousal on their level of teaching efficacy?

In addition, several secondary research questions will also be examined:

3. What is the difference in scores on the Teachers' Sense of Efficacy Scale (TSES) between pre-service teachers and those that have completed their in-service?

4. Do teachers with high levels of self-efficacy report different influences than teachers with low levels of self-efficacy?

Definition of Variables

This is a correlation study employing multiple regressions to explore the relationship between several independent variables and teacher efficacy (dependent variable). Figure 3 provides the definition for each of the variables used in the study; whether it is an independent or dependent variable; and an explanation of how the variable is being measured.

Research Question	Variable	Type	Definition	Measurement
1, 2, 3, and 4	Teacher Efficacy	Dependent	How competent does the Montessori pre-service teacher feel in his/her ability to affect the performance of all students?	Teacher Sense of Efficacy Scale (TSES)
1, 2, and 3	Mastery experience	Independent	Past successes create a strong sense of efficacy to accomplish similar future tasks, whereas, failures can lower one's efficacy perceptions particularly if they occur in the early stages of learning.	Teacher Sense of Efficacy Scale (TSES) Interview
1, 2, and 3	Vicarious experience	Independent	Level of support and relationship with mentor and its impact on level of effectiveness.	Teacher Sense of Efficacy Scale (TSES) Interview
1, 2, and 3	Verbal or social persuasion	Independent	Words of encouragement and moral support from others regarding one's performance may impact one's perceptions of efficacy.	Teacher Sense of Efficacy Scale (TSES) Interview
1, 2, and 3	Physiological arousal or emotional state	Independent	The impact of stress and anxiety on an individual's belief about their capabilities.	Teacher Sense of Efficacy Scale (TSES) Interview

Figure 1.6: Variables and how they are measured

It is important to understand how teacher self-efficacy is developed and maintained so that we can design educational interventions to prepare more effective teachers. Since this study focuses on the sources of teacher self-efficacy, the findings will supply invaluable knowledge based on the extent to which various source of efficacy information,(namely: mastery experience, vicarious experience, verbal persuasion, and physiological arousal) influence teacher self-efficacy during the pre-service year. This information will be beneficial to practitioners involved in the area of teacher preparation, such as supervising lecturers and mentor teachers, in providing a learning environment where pre-service teachers have opportunities to engage in experiences that foster high teacher self-efficacy. Furthermore, the findings may aid in designing meaningful and workable educational interventions aimed at strengthening teacher self-efficacy.

Introduction to the Chapters

In the current chapter, I outlined the purpose and significance of the study and the conceptual framework that supported my research. I stated the research questions and concluded this chapter with a brief overview of the study's methodology. This dissertation includes four additional chapters. Chapter 2 discusses and reviews the research and literature supporting a rationale for the study. Chapter 3 provides a detailed description of the methodology used for collecting and analyzing data, including the design, subjects, and sampling procedures. Chapter 4 discusses the administration of the research study and presents the findings in regard to the research questions. Finally, Chapter 5 addresses interpretations of the findings along with implications of the results

21

in the field of teacher preparation; projections for areas of further research; and limitations of the study.

CHAPTER 2

REVIEW OF THE LITERATURE

The purpose of this research study is to examine various sources influencing Montessori teachers' self-efficacy and the relative strength of those sources. This chapter will describe the components of social cognitive theory and self-efficacy as developed by Albert Bandura (1997), which establishes support those teachers with a strong perception of self-efficacy act in a particular way, contributing to students' academic performance and achievement. This will be followed by a historical overview of self-efficacy and the history and measurement of teacher self-efficacy. Finally, the Montessori pedagogy and its focus on the preparation of the teacher will be explored.

Social Cognitive Theory and Self-Efficacy

The concept of self-efficacy is grounded in the framework of social cognitive theory, which emphasizes the evolement and exercise of human agency (Bandura, 2006). It is generally defined as the belief in one's capabilities to achieve a goal or an outcome. Albert Bandura (1977) first introduced the cognitive social learning theory, which examines the human capacity to "exercise control over the nature and quality of one's life" (Bandura, 2001, p.1) through intentional actions. He proposed that the behavior a person exhibits is influenced by his or her beliefs regarding an outcome expectation and an efficacy expectation. In an outcome expectation, a person estimates that "a given behavior will lead to a certain outcome" (2001, p. 193). An efficacy expectation is the

23

belief a person has regarding his/her ability to actually perform the "behavior required to produce the outcome" (2001, p. 193). These two outcomes are distinct, particularly in the educational setting. While a teacher may believe that specific teacher behaviors will lead to a better classroom environment, improved student learning, increased class participation, and so on that same teacher may not have confidence in her ability to perform those behaviors. Efficacy beliefs determine how environmental opportunities and impediments are perceived (Bandura, 2006), and how they affect choice of activities; how much effort is expended on an activity; and how long people will persevere when confronting obstacles (Pajares, 1997).

Self-efficacy beliefs determine how people feel, think, behave, and motivate themselves; in the case of teachers this refers to the teacher's beliefs in their own ability to plan, organize, and carry out activities that are required to attain given educational goals. Bandura (1986, 1997) noted that behavior is more effectively predicted by the conviction that individuals have regarding their own capabilities than what they are actually capable of accomplishing. Therefore, an individual's self-belief is a driving force in his/her academic accomplishments. It is these ideas that determine "how well knowledge and skills are acquired" (Pajares, 2003, p.8).

Bandura further defines self-efficacy as judging one's ability to "produce desired results and forestall detrimental ones" (Bandura, 2001, p.10). These diverse effects arise from four major processes: intentionality; forethought; self-regulation; and self-reflectiveness. Intentionality is the ability of humans to choose a course of action,

24

whereas forethought implies setting goals, anticipating likely consequences, and choosing actions that are more likely to produce desired outcomes instead of undesirable outcomes. Self-regulation indicates the human ability to monitor the chosen choice of action through goal-setting and motivation. Finally, self-reflectiveness refers to the evaluation of the person's motivation, values, and meaning of the chosen action. A strong sense of efficacy enhances human accomplishment and personal well-being in many ways. A teacher, for example, with high confidence in her capabilities will approach difficult tasks as challenges to be mastered rather than as threats to be avoided. On the other hand, a teacher with a low level of self-efficacy will set incomplete goals, lose motivation and will not see herself as being competent and capable of the job. Although both these individuals may possess the same skills and knowledge to complete the task, their level of efficacy could mean they each perform the task in completely different manners (Bandura, 1993).

Bandura (1977) stated that people's conceptions of their self-efficacy, regardless accurate or misjudged, are developed through four sources of influence which he termed as (1) mastery experience or actual experience; (2) vicarious experience; (3) verbal or social persuasion; and (4) physiological arousal or emotional state. The first, and most effective, is through "mastery experiences," or successes at tasks (1994, p2). Mastery experiences increase one's self-efficacy, while failures may inhibit its development. The best mastery experiences should take time and effort to accomplish. Bandura (1977, 1997) identified vicarious experience as the second- most potent influence on one's sense of efficacy. Observing the successes of others similar to oneself contributes positively to self-efficacy. The opposite is also true – observing the failures of others similar to oneself

may decrease self-efficacy. Social persuasion is the words of encouragement or moral

support from others regarding one's performance that may modify one's perceptions of

efficacy. Self-efficacy can be influenced if told by others that they "have what it takes to

succeed" (1994, p.3). Self-efficacy can also be diminished if told by others they do not

possess the skills for success. Bandura believed that it was far easier for social persuasion

to decrease self-efficacy than to increase it (1994). Physiological and affective states

indicate the physical and mental processes that may interfere with the performance of the

task, such as exhaustion or anxiety. This is how people react to situations, whether

physical or mental. Typically, self-efficacy is boosted in a positive emotional state and

lowered in a negative emotional state (Bandura, 1997). These influences are affected by

four mental processes: cognitive; motivational; affective; and selection (Bandura, 1997).

Cognitive processes can enhance or inhibit the performance on the task through the self-

appraisal of one's capabilities. Motivation can affect efficacy through the establishment

of goals, while the ability to control negative emotional thoughts and to enhance positive

thoughts also has a strong impact on efficacy beliefs. Finally, selection refers to the

choices people make based on their efficacy beliefs.

Historical Overview of Self-Efficacy

At the turn of the 20th century, much attention was focused on the impact of

human behavior in relation to the idea of self. The American psychologist William James

believed that "introspective observation is what we have to rely on first and foremost and always" (1890, p.185). James was among the first psychologists to address "self-esteem" defining it as a feeling about one's self and what one thinks of personal accomplishments in relation to other members of society (Pajares, 2002).

Ivan Pavlov and B.F. Skinner dominated the 1920s to 1940s with their studies on stimuli and response and, as a result, the idea of "self "was waylaid. The educational field, which follows psychological theory, disregarded a focus on "self" as well. It was not until the 1950s that Abraham Maslow re-directed interest to the construct of self by addressing "motivational process" through his hierarchy of needs. In an effort to secure unsatisfied needs, an individual increase his motivation with "the need to become self-actualized, that is, to achieve one's potentialities, capacities and talents" (Pajares, 2002, p.3).

The work of Pavlov, Skinner, and Maslow gave birth to the humanistic movement in the 1960s and 1970s. By examining self-constructs and self-beliefs, schools tried to nurture self-esteem and a positive sense of self in their students. Much of the research on self-esteem and student achievement provided findings that were "inconclusive or provided unsettling results" (Pajares, 2002, p. 4) because these theories were not being realistically executed in the classroom. Understandably, following this, the enthusiasm towards understanding self-constructs diminished.

The 1970s and 1980s brought about the cognitive revolution, influenced greatly by technological advances such as the computer. Psychologists turned their attention to internal, mental tasking involving information procession, schema building, and problem solving. At the same time, a nationwide concern grew that academic standards were

27

dropping drastically and that students were being awarded a high school diploma bereft of necessary skills. This caused a "back to basics approach to curriculum and practice" in the educational system (Pajares, 2002).

Regardless of the momentary movement, Albert Bandura (1977) identified what he believed was an instrumental aspect missing from all the theories and educational reforms in his publication, *Self-efficacy: Toward a Unifying Theory of Behavioral Change*. Describing individuals as being perceptive of the capabilities that impact and help determine their choice of activities and persistence in reaching a goal, Bandura coined the term *self-efficacy*. In his 1986 publication, *Social Foundations of Thought and Action*, Bandura discussed a social cognitive theory in which he described people as having beliefs about their own capabilities. It is these beliefs (or self-perceptions) themselves, rather than their actual abilities are the driving force behind their achievements (Bandura, 1986, 1997; Pajares, 2002). Therefore, those who believe they have the capabilities to be successful make greater attempts to achieve the desired outcome.

We have seen that interest in beliefs about personal control and self-esteem has a long history in philosophy and psychology. It was Bandura who not only formalized the notion of perceived competence as self-efficacy, but offered a theory of how it develops and how it influences human behavior. From this point of view, namely, believing that you can accomplish what you set out to do, that many more theorists began to study the construct of self-efficacy.

28

What is Self-Efficacy?

Self-efficacy, as defined by Albert Bandura (1986), is "people's judgment of their capabilities to organize and execute courses of action required to attain designated types of performance" (p. 391). Bandura (1986) clarified that self-efficacy "is concerned not with the skills one has but with judgments of what one can do with whatever skills one possesses" (p.391). Perceived self-efficacy beliefs may impact a person in either a positive, empowering way, or in a negative, demoralizing way. How an individual believes s/he is able to carry out the necessary actions to achieve a desired result determines the course of action (Bandura, 1977): individuals who believe in their ability to perform a specific task will work harder and persist in order to successfully reach the goal than those who do not believe in their abilities. It is also important to note that efficacy levels are context and task specific, meaning the efficacy level for a proposed task may change within different contexts. For example, a person's efficacy level for teaching math may be high in a Montessori classroom of 'normalized' children (Montessori, 1989) but low in a classroom of children with special needs. In order to distinguish why self-efficacy levels differ, researchers must first have a thorough understanding of the sources of self-efficacy (Bandura, 2007).

Sources of Teacher Self-Efficacy

Bandura (1977) describes four sources of personal efficacy: performance accomplishments; vicarious experiences; verbal persuasions; and emotional arousals. The first source, mastery experience, refers to how individuals interpret their past performances. Performance accomplishments have the most potential for raising self-efficacy beliefs since they directly involve the individual and successful completion of a task. Bandura suggested that interpretations of past performance serve as a robust indicator of self-efficacy; this hypothesis has been supported by studies of the sources of students' self-efficacy (Usher & Pajares, 2008).

The experience gained by observing the successes and failures of others creates the second source, vicarious experience. In other words, when an individual observes someone else completing a similar task with success, it leads to the impression that they too could accomplish that task. Researchers propose that beginning teachers who have higher levels of induction support are more likely to view their jobs as manageable; report that they can teach the most difficult students, and indicate that they are successful in providing education to students needing special education services (Billingsley et al., 2004).

In addition to mastery and vicarious experiences, social or verbal persuasion also affects levels of self-efficacy. The persuasive messages individuals receive from others, such as; evaluative feedback from students, colleagues, administrators, and parents, likely influence how capable one feels in his job. Positive messages typically boost self-efficacy, while criticisms tend to undermine it. This is likely why teachers who perceive more support from their principals are less stressed and more committed and satisfied with their jobs than those who perceive less support (Billingsley & Cross, 1992). Similarly, research shows that educators who remain in their jobs were about four times more likely to recognize their administrators as supportive and encouraging than were the teachers who left their jobs (Boe, Barkanic, & Leow, 1999). Verbal persuasion thus allows an individual to overcome doubt when others express their beliefs in the individual's ability. Self-efficacy stemming from verbal persuasion is not enduring, however, and requires constant reassurance from others; any sign of failure or obstacles will weaken the individual's self-efficacy.

Physiological and emotional states, which deal with the individual's somatic and affective responses regarding his performance, are also a source of self-efficacy. For instance, excessive stress or anxiety can convince teachers they do not have the skills necessary to carry out his job successfully. Emotional arousal taps the individual's anxiety, steering him away from a feeling of avoidance. Teachers with low self-efficacy have reduced motivation to teach (Bandura, 1997). If the task is not successfully completed, the individual's self-efficacy will be further influenced in a negative manner (Bandura, 1977). On the other hand, those who feel energized by the teaching task likely approach their work with confidence. For example, the multiple pressures on special education teachers pose legitimate concerns for increased stress, which is associated with burnout and teacher attrition (Billingsley et al., 2004; Boyer & Gillespie, 2000). In general, self-efficacy will improve through consistently successful outcomes and decrease with repeated failures.

Bandura (1997) determines "Efficacy beliefs are best instilled by presenting the pursuit as relying on acquirable skills, raising performer's beliefs in their ability to

31

acquire skills, modeling the requisite skills, structuring activities in masterable steps that ensure a high level of initial success, and providing explicit feedback of continued progress (p. 105). Teachers' efficacy beliefs are best enhanced through the effective combination of efficacy information from different sources because each source of efficacy information alone may contribute in some way to the enhancement of teachers' efficacy beliefs (Labone, 2004). Thus, it is best for research investigating teachers' efficacy beliefs to consider the various sources of efficacy information.

After exploring the variables that influence student teachers' perceptions of their teaching efficacy, Mary Poulou (2007), highlighted the importance of student teachers' personality characteristics, capabilities, and motivation as potential sources of teaching efficacy. The author found that student teachers' motivation (for example, love for pupils, which enhances efforts towards effective teaching and personal effort and study about topics of teaching effectiveness) to improve their teaching efficacy received the highest ratings as a source of teaching efficacy in the study of 198 fourth-year students in Greece. In addition, student teachers' personality characteristics (for example, direct communication with pupils, positive stance/humor) and enactive mastery with social/verbal persuasion also received high mean scores as likely sources of teaching efficacy. Poulou mentioned that "the more student teachers perceived themselves as possessing specific personality characteristics and teaching capabilities, the more they felt efficacious in implementing instructional and discipline strategies and involving pupils in the learning process (p. 212).

In the longitudinal case study of one elementary science teacher during her transition from pre-service to in-service teaching, Mulholland and Wallace (2001) found that mastery experience was a powerful influence on her teaching confidence and perception of competence. In their case study of Katie, a beginning elementary school student teacher in Australia, the researchers noted that "the enthusiasm of children during a science lesson seemed to act as a form of social persuasion (Bandura, 1995) which encouraged Katie to teach science and had the potential to strengthen Katie's science teaching beliefs"(Mulholland & Wallace, 2001, p. 249). Mastery experiences were achieved when pre-service teachers were better able to use manageable manipulative and work with smaller groups of children who were interacting with other children. Early development of high self-efficacy beliefs by achieving mastery experiences is important to continue teaching science in the in-service situation. The authors found that the enthusiasm of children and social persuasion provided by children were the constant source of positive information in both pre-service and in-service situations, providing pressure to continue teaching science despite the setback. They emphasize the need to consider all sources of information in developing science teachers' self-efficacy because they recognize the lack of appropriate vicarious experience in the elementary school to be a major drawback to the development of science teaching self-efficacy. Charalambous, Philippou, and Kyriakides (2008) also found that it was important to observe, imitate, and analyze mathematics lessons taught by in-service teachers who were given vicarious experiences to student teachers in mathematics teaching. Thus, if self-efficacy is to be enhanced during pre-service teacher education, university-based education can provide

33

pre-service teachers with positive sources of vicarious experience offered by teacher educators' teaching modeling as well as discussion about teaching strategies (Mulholland & Wallace, 2001).

After analyzing four interviews, twelve written reflections, and seven transcribed group discussion, J.P. Rushton (2000) found that the five interns who spent eight months working in classrooms in inner-city schools moved past the cultural shock of their initial experiences and were able to teach more effectively. As the interns adjusted to the cultural differences, they came to accept the contrast between reality and their preconceptions, and grew better able to cope with them, they grew in efficacy. Each intern developed efficacy in different areas such as self-worth about becoming teachers, growth in relation to a sense of gaining authority and respect with pupils, and personal efficacy in relation to cooperating teachers. For example, one of the interns grew more patient in dealing with disruptive behavior after seeing her cooperating teachers' disciplinary strategies. In addition, the interns adopted their mentoring teacher's authoritarian approach to teaching, but did not become rigid, impersonal, arbitrary, and bureaucratic during their student teaching experiences (Rushton, 2000, 2003).

History and Measurement of Teacher Efficacy

Following the introduction of social cognitive theory and self-efficacy, researchers began exploring how these concepts could be used in the study of teaching and learning by identifying the construct of teacher efficacy and developing instrumentation to measure this construct. A teacher's belief that he possesses the ability

34

to influence student learning and achievement for all students, including those students who may be considered unmotivated and difficult, is commonly referred to as teacher self-efficacy (Bandura, 1977, 1997; Guske, 1987; Hoy, 2000). The development of a reliable and valid instrument that accurately measures teacher efficacy was of primary importance within this field of study and it was first introduced by the work of J.B. Rotter (1996). It was labeled the locus of control and was defined as "extent to which teachers believe that they could control the reinforcement of their actions, that is, whether the control reinforcement lay within themselves or in the environment" (Tschannen-Moran et al., 1998, p.202). The locus of control is the perception of where one's behavior stems (Rotter, 1996). There are two distinct paths of locus of control: external and internal control. External control is the belief that reward is due to luck, fate, chance or higher powers. Internal control is the belief that behaviors and actions are a result of personal characteristics.

The RAND corporation researchers were the first to use locus of control to measure teacher self-efficacy. In 1977, the Rand Corporation studied planned change over a period of four years; this "Change Agent Study" looked closely at the change process and teacher growth. Rand researchers included items that explored the perceived ability of teachers to control their actions and environment. Interestingly, teacher efficacy was the most significant teacher attribute to growth and change throughout these studies (Rand, 1977, No VII). It was found that teachers who identified themselves as highly efficacious "believed they could control or strongly influence student achievement and motivation" (Tschannen-Moran et al., 1998, p. 202). Those teachers possessing a low sense of teacher self-efficacy believed environmental factors played a bigger role in outcomes than their actions. These teachers believed that environmental factors or external factors such as "conflict, violence, or substance abuse…" affected student's learning more than their own influence (Tschannen-Moran et al., 1998, p. 204).

Using Rotter's locus of control theory, the RAND researchers first measured teacher self-efficacy through two items in a questionnaire. The items were:

RAND Item 1: When it comes right down to it, a teacher really can't do much because most of a student's motivation and performance depends on his or her home environment (Tschannen-Moran et al., 1998).

This item was labeled general teaching efficacy and reflects agreement with an external locus of control.

RAND Item 2: If I really try hard, I can get through to even the most difficult or unmotivated students. (Tschannen-Moran et al., 1998).

This item has been labeled personal teaching efficacy and indicates agreement with an internal locus of control.

The RAND researchers discovered the scores on these two items, the teacher's sense of efficacy, had impacts on student motivation, stress level, teacher's willingness to implement innovation, and teacher's willingness to stay in the field. These two items consequently became the basis and inspiration for teacher efficacy instruments developed by various researchers. Later research by McLaughlin and Marsh (1978) found teacher efficacy to positively impact: achievement of a project goal; the amount of adjustment made by the teacher throughout the project; student achievement; and, continued use of project methods and materials (McLaughlin & Marsh, 1978; Symlie, 1990).

Supporting the construct of teacher efficacy are the indirect investigations by Brookover et al. in 1978, and Brophy and Evertson in 1977. Brookover et al. (1978) studied social-psychological variables that set schools of similar socioeconomic standards and racial composition apart, based on students' academic performance. According to the study, teachers who demonstrate a great instructional commitment to students and practice positive reinforcement, nurture higher-achieving students (Brookover et al, 1978).

Using Rotter's Theory and the RAND items as a base, other researchers developed instruments with the hope of effectively measuring teacher self-efficacy. Rose and Medway (1981) developed a measure called the Teacher Locus of Control (TLC). The TLC is a 28-item questionnaire 'where teachers were asked to assign responsibility of student success/failure by choosing between two competing explanations for the situations described" (Tschannen-Moran et al., 1998, p. 206). Rose and Medway found the responses to the TLC were weakly but significantly related to the RAND items. Another instrument measuring Responsibility for Student Achievement (RSA) was also discovered in 1981 by T. R. Guskey. Guskey(1984) found strong inter-correlations between overall responsibility and responsibility for student success/failure as well as a relation between positive attitudes about teaching to greater efficacy levels.

During the same time that instruments were being created based on Rotter's theory and the RAND items, other researchers were creating instruments based on Bandura's (1977) self-efficacy theory. Building on the distinction between "personal teaching efficacy' (PTE) and "general teaching efficacy" (GTE) laid out in the RAND Study, Dembo and Gibson (1984) made links to Bandura's outcome expectancy concept. They began with modifications to the RAND items and incorporated Bandura's theory. In 1984, Gibson and Dembo created the most popular measure thus far, the Teacher Efficacy Scale (TES), which proposes to capture Bandura's two elements of efficacy, efficacy expectation and outcome expectancy, by having participants respond to statements such as "when a student gets a better grade than he usually gets, it is usually because I found better ways of teaching" and "even a teacher with good teaching abilities may not reach many students." PTE relates to "levels of organization, planning, and fairness a teacher displayed as well as clarity and enthusiasm in teaching" (Tschannen-Moran et al., 1998, p. 213). GTE is assumed to measure outcome expectancy and is related to clarity and enthusiasm in teacher (Tschannen-Moran et al., 1998). The Gibson-Dembo instrument uses a 5-point Likert scale ranging from 1 (strongly disagree) to 5 (strongly agree) and became the dominant measure of teacher efficacy for twenty years. It was found that teacher self-efficacy influences student's attitudes toward school, subjects, teachers, and new ideas (Tschannen-Moran et al., 1998) and that students in second and

38

fifth grade whose teachers had a higher sense of GRT outperformed their peers in math on the Iowas Test of Basic Skills (Moore & Esselman, 1992).

Dissatisfaction with the definition and measurement of the two sub-constructs called for a new instrument that must "encompass both an assessment of personal competence and an analysis of the task in terms of the resources and constraints that exist in particular teaching contexts" (Tschannen-Moran, et al., 1998, p. 240). The instruments failed to meet both criteria and a new instrument was needed to be specific enough to have good reliability, yet general enough to avoid losing predictive power. Soodak and Podell (1996) argued that teacher efficacy was actually a three dimensional construct consisting of personal efficacy, outcome efficacy, and teaching efficacy. Using the TES, they added additional items and through factor analysis, identified the three sub-constructs. They defined personal efficacy as a teacher's belief that she has the necessary teaching skills; outcome efficacy as the belief that when the teaching skills are used they produce a desired student outcome; and teaching efficacy was defined as the belief that teachers can overcome the effects of all outside influences on their students. Emmer and Hickman (1991) asserted that teachers spend a considerable amount of time managing student behaviors and therefore the quality of this management may lead to feelings of high or low efficacy. They modified the TES to include the sub-construct of classroom management with two sub-constructs of PTE and GTE sub-constructs.

Although these studies attempted to strengthen the construct of teacher efficacy, they relied on a poorly designed instrument that did not completely capture the

39

complexity of Bandura's theory of self-efficacy. Therefore, researchers began the work of redefining and remodeling the construct of measuring teacher efficacy. Tschannen-Moran sought to develop a new instrument based on the previous recommendations that stated a reliable and valid instrument for measuring teacher self-efficacy did not exist (Tschannen-Moran et.al., 1998). The development of a new instrument began by deciding to follow and expand recommendations set by Bandura. They introduced a new conceptual model of teacher efficacy that demonstrates the cyclical and context- specific nature of this construct. The conceptual model cognitively processes Bandura's four sources of efficacy information (mastery experiences, physiological and emotional states, vicarious experiences, and social persuasion), and then either analyses the teaching task or assesses the personal teaching competence. The processes result in a level of teacher efficacy that determines teaching performance, which becomes a new source of efficacy information in itself. However, the instrument had issues with construct validity and Denzine, Cooney, and McKenzie (2005) determined that the TES did not accurately fit Bandura's model of social learning theory.

Therefore, researchers began work on developing new instruments with stronger construct validity. In response to the issues presented above in the measurement of teacher efficacy, Bandura (1997) demonstrated that self-efficacy and locus of control have little or no statistical relationship between each other. Reacting to the generality of the above mentioned measures and to the lack of correlation with locus of control, Bandura (undated) presented his own 30 item measure that recognizes the differing tasks that teachers may be asked to perform. The scale is measured on a 9 point Likert scale which details the amount of influence a teacher believes they exert over the stated situation. While this scale is more conceptually specific and task oriented, the teaching tasks which are included have been criticized for not representing normal teaching activities (Tschannen-Moran & Woolfolk Hoy, 2001). There is no reliability and validity evidence available for this scale. Roberts and Henson (2000) developed an efficacy instrument that attempts to address the theoretical and methodological issues associated with the TES for use with science education teachers. Friedman and Kass (2002) also suggested a model of teacher efficacy that accounts for the teacher's school context and her relationships in the school.

Using the conceptual models of Tschannen-Moran and Woolfolk and Hoy (2001) developed a new way to measure teacher efficacy, the Teacher's Sense of Efficacy Scale (TSES). The instrument was designed to evaluate "both personal competence and an analysis of the task in terms of the resources and constraints in particular teaching contexts" (2001, p.795). TSES attempts to further define normal teaching tasks and to broaden the focus from unmotivated students to include capable students. The sub-constructs of efficacy for instructional strategies; efficacy for classroom management; and efficacy for student engagement include questions such as: "To what extent can you use a variety of assessment strategies?" and "How much can you do to control disruptive behavior in the classroom?" It was developed and refined in three studies. From those studies, three factors emerged that accounted for over half of the variance. Those factors were labeled Efficacy for Student Engagement, Efficacy for Instructional Practices, and Efficacy for Classroom Management. In keeping to the recommendations for a specific,

41

yet general instrument, Tschannen-Moran et al. (1998) believed the student engagement, instructional practices, and classroom management were three common elements that any teacher would face. This procedure resulted in two versions of the instrument, a 24 -item long version; and a 12- item short version. Both scales use the nine-point Likert-type response scale with the options 1 (nothing), 3 (very little), 5 (some influence), 7 (quite a bit), and 9 (a great deal). Factor analysis then confirmed the existence of the three factors that accounted for 54 percent of the variance in the long form, and 65percent in the short form. Finally, second-order analysis revealed that measures could conform to one factor alone, which explained 75 percent of the variance in the long form and 68 percent of the variance in the short form. Item loadings were appropriate for the three subscales and the one entire scale. Internal reliabilities ranged from .87 to .91. The TSES is "superior to previous measures of teacher efficacy in that it has a unified and stable factor structure and assesses a broad range of capabilities that teachers consider important to good teaching…" (Tschannen-Moran et al., 2001).This scale has the potential to fully capture the efficacy expectation and outcome expectancy sub-constructs that are at the heart of Bandura's self-efficacy theory, but additional research utilizing this instrument - along with confirmatory qualitative analysis - is needed to ensure the validity of this measure (Henson, 2002).

This scale seems to have the potential to fully capture the efficacy expectation and outcome expectancy sub-constructs that are at the heart of Bandura's self-efficacy theory, but additional research is needed to ensure the validity of this measure. Roberts and Henson (2001) used confirmatory factor analysis to examine the initial version of the

TSES, but did not find sufficient support for the sub-construct Efficacy for Student Engagement (ESE); they recommended the construct be either strengthened or eliminated. Tschannen-Moran and Woolfolk Hoy decided to strengthen the ESE sub-construct so the final version demonstrated adequate reliability and validity (Tschannen-Moran et al., & Woolfolk Hoy, 2001). Heneman, Kimball, and Milanowski (2006) reported on a validation study of the TSES in which the sample produced valid and reliable data and included all levels of teachers in its pool. They also determined that teacher scores on the TSES significantly predicted teacher performance ratings at the end of the school year. Whereas major strides have been made, it is clear that there are still issues to be addressed in this research field. Perhaps a mixture of qualitative and quantitative methods would be the logical choice in studying teacher efficacy.

Self-Efficacy and Student Achievement

Albert Bandura studied self-efficacy in relation to a variety of factors, such as motivation (Schunk, 1994) and phobias (Bandura, 1983). He noted that individuals develop ideas and self-perceptions about their capabilities, which, in turn, "drive" an individual's interaction with his environment. Bandura (1977) refers to this control as "perceived self-efficacy." Three studies explored the relationship between teacher efficacy and student achievement; all of which supported the conclusion that teachers with higher levels of efficacy appear to produce higher- achieving students. First, Rose and Medway (1981) used the Teacher Locus of Control (TLC) scale, which measures efficacy through an internal versus external orientation with a sample of 17 teachers and

43

their students. Internally - oriented teachers attribute consequences to their own actions, while externally-oriented teachers attribute consequences to factors outside their control. The scores from the TLC measure, teacher observations, and student achievement data allowed the researchers to determine that teachers with high levels of internal attribution did have higher achieving students. Next, Ashton, Webb, & Doda (1983) used a sample of 48 modestly-skilled high school teachers to explore student achievement data, teacher efficacy scores from the two Rand items, and classroom observations. Their results indicate levels of teaching efficacy are positively correlated to student achievement in mathematics and language arts. Ross (1992) also found a positive relationship between student achievement and teacher efficacy by observing the effect of coaching on teacher efficacy and student achievement. The researcher worked with eighteen history teachers and six instructional coaches to track student achievement as they implemented a new curriculum. Using the TES, student tests, coaching survey, and interviews, the results illustrated that student achievement increased significantly from pre-test to pos-test. All these studies demonstrate a strong positive relationship between student achievement and teacher efficacy; additional research involving the TSES and further examining the impact of high level teacher efficacy is needed though.

In recognizing that efficacy belief is context specific, researchers developed scales that focused on specific content areas, such as Riggs and Enochs' (1990) Science Teaching Efficacy Belief Instrument (STEBI) (which was refined by Enochs' and Riggs (1990) into the STEBI-B); and Enochs, Smith, and Huinker's (2000) Mathematics Teaching Efficacy Beliefs Instrument (MTEBI). Both of these instruments rework the

44

statements on the TES from a more general teaching focus to a precise science or mathematics teaching focus, employing questions such as, "I understand science concepts well enough to be effective in teaching elementary science," and "When a student does better than usual in mathematics, it is often because the teacher exerted a little extra effort." These scales retained the five-point Likert scoring of the TES as well as the low validity issues, with both scales explaining less than 30 percent of the variance in teacher efficacy.

Other studies have specifically investigated variable related to the sense of efficacy in teachers. Emmer and Hickman (1991) proposed a new dimension to teacher efficacy: efficacy in classroom management and discipline. The authors asserted that teachers spend a considerable amount of time managing student behaviors, the quality of which may, lead to feelings of high or low efficacy. The researchers added items to the TES that reflected classroom management and disciplinary situations. Using factor analysis, the final instrument revealed three factors: classroom management/discipline; external influences; and personal teaching efficacy.

A study involving twenty elementary school children from Los Angeles participating in the preferred reading program focused on the classroom practices of those who successfully improved reading scores. Teacher efficacy, identified as "their sense of being able to get through to students, their commitment and morale" (p. 38) positively affected black children's reading scores (Armor, et.al., 1976). Another study, connecting teacher self-efficacy to student achievement was executed by Berman, et al (1977), in which two middle schools with different organizational variables believed to impact teacher efficacy were reviewed. After four or five classroom observations, the authors concluded, "our study of teacher efficacy beliefs indicates that the extent to which teachers believe they are capable of influencing student performance affects their enthusiasm and persistence in working with their students and ultimately their students' achievement" (Ashton, et. al., 1982, p.11).

In short, teachers who possess stronger perceptions of self-efficacy tend to display specific observable behaviors, such as effort, persistence, enthusiasm, and confidence. These teachers manage classroom time differently and engage students in learning for longer periods of time. Teachers with strong self-efficacy exemplify warmth and responsiveness to all students, especially those with reduced abilities. As David Kearns (1988) acknowledged, failing to change the willingness of every teacher to have a positive impact on every student and failing to inspire teachers to believe in their own abilities, is failing to deal with a critical educational issue. It is imperative that teachers believe in themselves and their students if educational strides are to be made.

Recently, research studies have focused on the influence of teacher efficacy beliefs on general classroom teaching practices. For instance, teacher self-efficacy is associated with quality of instruction and the use of innovative teaching methods (Tschannen-Moran & Woolfolk Hoy, 2001). Teachers confident in their capabilities not only report less stress, but also remain in the teaching profession longer with a greater commitment than do teachers who doubt their capabilities (Schwarzer & Hallum, 2008;

Ware & Kitsantas, 2007). In other words, teacher self-efficacy serves as a defensive factor for burn-out which has been a constant problem in the teaching profession. Furthermore, compared to teachers with low self-efficacy, teachers with increased self-efficacy display the following methods of avoiding stress: use more effective instructional strategies; manage classroom behavior more effectively; exert more effort in organizing, planning, and delivering their lessons; set higher goals for instruction; and engage students to a greater extent in learning compared to teachers with low self-efficacy (Allinder, 1994; Chwalitsz, Altameyer & Russel, 1992; Ross, 1998; Tschannen-Moran & Woolfolk Hoy, 2001).Additionally, teachers who display more confidence in their skills are typically more receptive to the consultation and application of novel instructional practices (Morrison, Wakefield, Walker, & Solberg, 1994); teachers with low self-efficacy direct more frequent criticism toward students making mistakes, and are more susceptible to becoming frustrated when classroom routines are not followed (Gibson & Dembo, 1984; Woolfolk, Rosoff, & Hoy, 1990).

While studies demonstrate direct links between a teacher's perceived self-efficacy and student achievement, various factors within the school system impact that perception as well. Researchers have thus turned their attention toward investigating the origins of teacher efficacy beliefs for important insights on fostering self-efficacy during teacher training (Henson, 2002; Labone, 2004; Woolfolk Hoy, 2002). In spite of this growing body of research, it is unclear how well these findings generalize to teachers of different student populations.

47

Teacher Preparation and Induction

Scholars have also explored the impact of teacher preparation programs and novice teacher induction on teacher efficacy levels. This includes the effect of teaching on levels of efficacy; the durability and changes from methods classes to student teaching to the first year of teaching; and the method of instruction for teacher preparation. Although a few studies have found some variability in the pattern, these studies indicate teacher efficacy levels generally increase during methods courses and student teaching.

Volkman, Scheffler, and Dana (1992) examined, two groups of pre-service elementary teachers completing their student teaching experiences, and discovered several differences amongst them. The first group of 12 pre-service teachers was placed in an environment that encouraged reflective practices. They were given one-on-one meetings with a supervisory teacher, and met bi-weekly with the other students in the treatment group for more reflective practice activities. The remaining 12 pre-service teachers were placed in one of two control schools with no emphasis on reflective practices. Each of the participants was asked to complete a journal reflecting on their experience during this period, and to complete the TES prior to student teaching and after student teaching. Using ANCOVA with post-test TES scores as the dependent variable, pre-test TES scores as the covariate, and the treatment group as the independent variable, the results indicated the treatment group had significantly higher levels of teacher efficacy than the control group. The qualitative analysis of the journal entries supported the results and revealed the treatment group's entries were more reflective and insightful in general.

Another study investigating the benefits of student teaching place 100 pre-service teachers in different settings, but did not separate them into a treatment or control group (Fortman and Pontius 2000).The students were asked to complete a modified version of the TES prior to student teaching, at the midpoint of student teaching, and at the end of student teaching. Using a paired t-test, PTE post-test scores were significantly higher than pre-test scores; scores on GTE were lower from pre-test to post-test, but not considerably. The results also argued that females scored much higher than males on both pre-test and post-test PTE scores. Along with the Volkman, Scheffler, and Dana (1992) study, these findings show student teaching has a positive impact on levels of efficacy.

Several other studies have explored the trend of efficacy levels from methods courses to student teaching and beyond, but have found somewhat conflicting results.Woolfolk Hoy and Spero (2005) tracked levels of teacher efficacy in 53 pre-service teachers from the beginning of their teacher preparation to the end of student teaching, and then at the end of their first year of teaching. The participants were asked to complete three different measures of teacher efficacy: the TES; Bandura's scale; and a newly developed Ohio State Teaching Confidence Scale. The results clarified that levels of teacher efficacy increased from the beginning of teacher preparation to the end of student teaching on all three measures. Between the end of student teaching and the end of the first year of teaching, efficacy levels notably decreased on Bandura's scale and the GTE scale. The OSU scale demonstrated relatively stable scores.

Moreover, Palmer (2006) examined the efficacy levels of 55 pre-service teachers at the beginning of a science methods course, at the end of the course, and at the end of the program, using the STEBI-B and interview data from 18 of the participants. A repeated-measures ANOVA revealed teacher efficacy increased significantly between the beginning of the methods course and the end of the methods course. There were no important differences between the post-test scores and the delayed post-test scores administered at the end of the program, thus the gains in efficacy remained stable across time and student teaching. As supported by the interviews, all the participants felt positive about teaching science.

In a similar vein, Fives, Hamman, and Olivarez (2007) assessed the trend in teacher efficacy during student teaching to determine whether teacher burnout characteristics could be revealed this early on. The 49 participants were asked to complete the TSES and other surveys measuring teacher burnout and learning questionnaires before and after student teaching. Using a MANOVA with the three factors from the TSES (efficacy for instructional practices; efficacy for student engagement; and efficacy for classroom management) as the dependent variables, all three factors showed considerable increases from pre-test to post-test.

In order to explore how efficacy levels are impacted by various school and personal factors, Chester and Beaudin (1996) surveyed a group of 173 newly-hired

50

teachers in urban schools. This group of teachers included both novice teachers in general, and experienced teachers new to a school. Again, a TES administered at the beginning and at the end of the school year was used. The intent was to evaluate independent variables of teacher placement; opportunity to collaborate; attention supervisors pay to performance; and the availability and quality of resources. Evidently, teacher efficacy increased in older novice teachers but decreased in younger novice teachers. Efficacy levels tended to decline for overall experienced, newly -hired teachers who reported high levels of collaboration, and who reported a high number of observations.

Picking up on the student teaching aspect of teacher efficacy, Chambers (2003) questioned whether the length of student teaching produced changes in teacher efficacy. Surveying 28 pre-service teachers enrolled in a two semester student teaching program and 27 pre-service teachers enrolled in a one semester student teaching program, she examined group differences in the TES. A *t*-test statistic and multiple regression statistics were computed, but disclosed no differences between the two groups regarding efficacy level. Therefore, the duration of student teaching may not create any differences in levels of teacher efficacy.

Finally, Gorrell and Capron (1987) examined a group of 86 pre-service teachers with low- to- moderate levels of teacher efficacy to determine whether different instructional methods shaped varying levels of efficacy. Pre-service teachers were initially given the Potential Teacher's Attitude Questionnaire (PTAQ) as a measure of efficacy, from which low-scoring students and moderate-scoring students were placed into two groups. The first group received direct instructions on a teaching task, followed by a student teacher demonstrating how to employ the task with a student and discussing the instructions. The second group received cognitive modeling instructions for completing the teaching task, followed by a student teacher demonstrating the task with a student while employing cognitive modeling thought processes. The pre-service teachers were then given the PTAQ again to compare scores. The low efficacy group/direct instruction group had higher levels of efficacy than the low efficacy/cognitive modeling group, but the moderate efficacy/cognitive modeling group had higher levels of efficacy than the moderate efficacy/direct instruction group. Consequently, a direct instruction approach might be more effective in elevating low-efficacy teachers.

All in all, the pattern of efficacy seems to increase during teacher preparation, but decreases during student teaching in some cases. While certain studies efficacy levels may decrease during the first year of teaching, other factors could mediate that decline. Unfortunately, fully understanding the conditions that heighten or dampen efficacy levels requires additional research. Furthermore, scholars should also consider assessing changes in efficacy scores for initial low-to-moderate scoring teachers, as the initial high scoring teachers should not have much variability. Although these studies do guide student teaching duration and instructional methods for low-efficacy teachers, more work with a common instrument is needed to verify these findings. This study focuses on teachers within preschools following the Montessori Method of education.

Maria Montessori and her Legacy

As the first woman to practice medicine in Italy, Dr. Maria Montessori spent time working with children in the slums of Rome and quickly became interested in their development. Her scientific observations of this group laid the foundation of a highly organized pedagogy (2006) that has flourished worldwide. This visionary pedagogy did not, however, emerge in isolation; Montessori perused Jean Itard, Johann Pestalozzi, Leo Tolstoy, Friedrich Froebel, Johann Herbart, and William James and crossed paths with Anna Freud, Erik Erikson, and Jean Piaget. Her writings alluded to the work of naturalists, evolutionists, philosophers, theosophist, public leaders, and ancient thinkers. Montessori's ideas extended to almost every major field of knowledge, and evolved into a framework of human development from birth to childhood. This is a framework for collaboration, invention and discovery that is unlimited in possibilities, yet fixed and coherent at the same time.

A revolutionary/radical by nature, by nature, Montessori sought educational reform as the vehicle *par excellence* for the regeneration of mankind. She developed her pedagogy with the intention of promoting the natural ability of children to focus and sustain their attention, a capacity which initiates a transition from capricious and disorderly toward self- disciplined in the child's temperament (1989). Her teaching methods were based on her observations of how children learned best; in this way she avoided a search for patterns of child development that conformed to adult ideals of how children should behave. As a result, Montessori paradoxically discovered that, given the right environment and stimulation, a child could develop behavior and achievements beyond all expectations. She realized children are better learners before six years of age than they will ever be again, and that they could learn almost anything through special techniques.

Montessori's interest in pedagogy grew from her work with children who were categorized as *deficient* or *idiots* (Kramer, 1978*)*. Her search for pedagogical treatment for intellectual deficiency led her to the French doctors, Jean Itard and Eduard Seguin. Itard's *Wild Boy of Averyon* (1801) dramatically confirmed the importance of the young child's environment, while Itard's student, Seguin, pioneered work with handicapped children that provided Montessori with more direct help in her early years of teaching. She used many of the materials Seguin developed, including the grooved letters that would later to become the "sandpaper letters", and the Seguin Boards that taught number concepts. The work of these two doctors inspired academic approach centered on a child's purposeful activity, generated through interaction with carefully-designed learning materials. By the end of her life, Montessori's pedagogy was a comprehensive array of didactic objects and accompanying exercises designed to capture and to hold children's attention. Montessori's observations convinced her that children's spontaneous interest in, and subsequent extended interaction with, these didactic objects resulted in intellectual and social development.

By testing new approaches and materials and noting children's reactions, Dr. Montessori developed a radically different system of education. The pedagogy presents the content of educational knowledge as a system of relations linking the major disciplines (including language study, mathematics, geometry, history, geography, science, music, and the visual arts) to the interests and needs of the developing child, from early childhood to adolescence. This system was developed by trial and error over her lifetime, with children in places as diverse as Rome and Chennai.

Though Montessori's contributions to the field of early childhood education are often mentioned in university textbooks, the underlying theories that guided her work receive little discussion. Her approach has been diluted to represent a variety of doctrines, including education in the tradition of Rousseau (Postman, 1999); progressive education in the vein of Dewey (McDermott, 1962); genetic epistemology resembling Piaget (Elkind, 1974); the transition from modernist to post-modernist views of childhood and constructivism (Elkind, 2003); and social development theory akin to Vygotsky (Bodrova, 2003). Although valid, this diverse selection does not fully realize the intricacies of the Montessori Method. Comprehending Montessori's philosophy is particularly challenging as it stems from an oral body of work largely unavailable to scholars unless they attend a formal Montessori teacher training program.

The Prepared Adult

Montessori believed that "the first step in the integral resolution of the problem of education must not, therefore, be taken toward the child, but toward the adult educator. He must change his moral attitudes. He must divest himself of many preconceptions" (1989, p. 20). In her extensive writings, Montessori provides in-depth clarification pertaining to the desired qualities of the prepared adult (teacher). Her ideas concerning the active nature of learning suggest a model in which the teacher does not directly cause understanding in students, but rather prepares the environment and removes impediments to knowledge. This would require that adults were prepared for the task for whereas

> it is true that the child develops in his environment through activity itself, but he needs material means, guidance and an indispensable understanding. It is the adult who provides these necessities….If (the adult) does less than is necessary, the child cannot act meaningfully, and if he does more than is necessary, he imposes himself upon the child, extinguishing (the child's) creative impulses. (Montessori, 1989, p.154)

Although the teacher oversees the Montessori classroom, it is truly the child's classroom, with everything scaled to and arranged for the children. "Whereas traditionally teachers are thought to have as a main role the imparting of knowledge, in Montessori education the teacher's main role is connecting the child to the environment, in part through giving lessons, and in part by maintaining the environment" (Lillard, 2005, p. 282). The teacher's task is thus to prepare the materials but to refrain 'from obtrusive interference' in the children's activity (1946, p. 3). Montessori emphasized that "education is not what the teacher gives; education is a natural process spontaneously carried out by the human individual, and is acquired not by listening to words but by experiences upon the environment" (1946, p.3).

In addition to a proven way of engaging individuals in learning, that is successful because it follows the natural development of the child, the Montessori approach encompasses a vital intrinsic ingredient – the attitude, mannerisms, and knowledge of the prepared adult. This particular and different role for the teacher, Montessori maintained,

56

required extensive training. Whereas traditional teacher training focuses on assessments, and curricula, classroom management, Montessori teacher training includes both personal preparation and instructions in the lessons and the materials.

Preparation of the Montessori Teacher

Since a comprehensive record of the materials and activities that constitute the Montessori pedagogy are not found in any published source, the training of Montessori teachers is an oral training. A combination of lectures, hands-on practice with the materials, album-writing, and oral examination has been transmitting the method since 1913, when Montessori delivered a training course in Rome (Kramer, 1976).

Moreover though, Montessori teachers must undergo through extensive training in both preparing themselves personally and in learning the Montessori philosophy and methodology. Inner preparation should not be seen as effortless or as resulting in an immediate transformation, but as requiring a lifetime of deep reflection and passionate commitment. Furthermore, the ability to observe children and to detect their needs is fundamental to good Montessori teaching, which Montessori assessed must be carefully developed through long practice (1917). Interestingly, she was convinced a background in traditional education would hinder one from being a high-quality Montessori teacher: "An ordinary teacher cannot be transformed into a Montessori teacher, but must be created anew; having rid herself of pedagogical prejudices" (Montessori, 1963, p. 87). Even if a "system of countervailing motions that contains a remarkably hearty balance, an equilibrating process that continually manufactures an immunity to change" (Kegan and

Lahey, 2001, p. 6) exists, Montessori teachers must avoid reverting to old patterns and traditional methods of education. In order not to go back to previous ways, we must be aware and conscious all the time that old habits die hard. Change requires effort. Kegan and Lahey (2001) discuss how individuals have a powerful inclination not to change and how "the processes of dynamic equilibrium, which, like an immune system, powerfully and mysteriously tend to keep things pretty much as they are" (p.5). Inner preparation cannot be seen as effortless or resulting in an immediate transformation. It requires a lifetime of both deep reflection and passionate commitment.

Montessori also felt it was important for children to be around teachers with a certain level of maturity and spiritual self-awareness. She knew that children absorb not only the words and actions of those around them, but also their energetic qualities. Montessori insisted "on the fact that a teacher must prepare himself interiorly by systematically studying himself so that he can tear out his most deeply rooted defects, those in fact which impede his relations with children….A good teacher does not have to be entirely free from faults and weaknesses (but should know what they are)" (Montessori, 1966, p. 149). Since the preparation of a Montessori teacher involves personal change to eschew becoming an obstacle to the child's growth, she must confront her own prejudices; only then will she be able to observe the child clearly.

Montessori in her lectures and texts documented both strengths of the adult character that would aid the child, and weaknesses of disposition that would act as an impediment to development. Although many other educational approaches now acknowledge the critical importance of the early, formative years, no other teacher training seems to place great emphasis on the inner preparation of the adult. It is almost as though this critical aspect of an adult's character is outside the realm of educational discussions.

In addition to personal preparation, a Montessori teacher should have a strong knowledge base of the Montessori materials and their presentation. These materials have been designed to capture and to hold the attention of a child, and they accordingly have a history, a context, and a pedagogic motivation. Each has a specific way of being presented and students in training learn about these materials and the many ways they can be used to stimulate interest, as well as their connections to different areas of the curriculum. During their internship, student teachers practice with these materials in front of children as they must show a strong understanding of them during a practical examination. Montessori (1963) countered the superficial presumption that her method requires too little of the teacher by stating "when the didactic material is considered, its quantity and the order and details of its presentation, the task of the teacher becomes both active and complex….Her later "inactivity" is a sign of her success" (p. 86).

A Practitioner's Perspective

Although Montessori provided a strong methodology to support her philosophy of education, sadly, not all Montessori school practice the method as it was originally intended. At present, there are approximately 4000 Montessori schools in North America and thousands more around the world (Lillard, 2005). Since the Montessori Method was

59

never trademarked, and because it lacks a governing organization, there is tremendous diversity within the community of "Montessori" schools. Unlike the Primrose or KinderCare franchises, no two Montessori schools are the same: some pride themselves on remaining faithful to their interpretation of Montessori's original vision, while others simply use the name and nothing else.

While every school community certainly has its merits, the lack of acute understanding about the Montessori philosophy is unfortunate indeed. For instance, many schools fill their classrooms with Montessori materials but neglect the "free choice, the organization and order, the collaborative learning and interaction" (Lillard, 2005, p. 330) aspects. Montessori, on the other hand, thought children learned best when they are allowed freedom in a setting that has been carefully prepared for them. Another issue plaguing the Montessori community is that "it is hard for people to abandon culturally transmitted ideas about children and schooling, and Montessori teachers often adopt traditional school practices because those practices feel familiar (to parents and to themselves) and seem, on the surface, to work." (Lillard, 2005, p.329). Furthermore, the contrast between a traditional and Montessori teacher seems very minute to an undiscerning eye, so many "Montessori" teachers are not properly trained in the method. Self- directed internships, condensed training programs, and prewritten lesson plans all reduce "the depth of the Montessori philosophy and the vast array of interconnections between the materials and the philosophy" (Lillard, 2005, p.220). In effect, these shortcomings hinder a teacher's self-efficacy as they lack the resources to implement the Montessori pedagogy.

60

Conclusion

The range of theories on teacher efficacy becomes particularly important in light of Montessori's emphasis on the personal preparation of the teacher. Unfortunately, despite searches on various databases (including Google Scholar, JSTOR and Wilson Web) no empirical studies of Montessori teachers or Montessori teacher preparation were found. In this study, I will draw on the elements of teacher support and school environment; retention and coping mechanisms; attitudes and awareness; and instructional methods to scrutinize the sources pertinent to self-efficacy. I will base my research on Tschannen-Moran and Woolfolk Hoy's Teacher's Sense of Efficacy Scale (TSES), as this is the best instrument to evaluate Bandura's levels of self-efficacy. Although this body of work is certainly valid it was evident that the sources of teacher self-efficacy themselves merited more attention; therefore, I undertook a study to better understand how these beliefs are conceived and nurtured. As Pavlov's work contributed to insights on self esteem, this research should contribute to professional development and teacher preparation programs.

CHAPTER 3

METHODOLOGY

Introduction

The purpose of this study was to examine various sources influencing Montessori pre-service teachers' self-efficacy and the relative strength of these sources of influence on Montessori teachers' self-efficacy. The study was designed to predict the influences, add to the current knowledge base, have a personal, social and organizational impact upon the teaching profession, and gain a deeper understanding of a complex phenomenon. It was carried out in two phrases. Both quantitative and qualitative methods were employed throughout the investigation to enhance the credibility of the data (Goodwin & Goodwin, 1996). I was able to achieve triangulation by using different methods to assess similar constructs and enable data expansion by broadening the depth of the inquiry used (Goodwin & Goodwin, 1996; Miles & Huberman, 1994).To put it simply, "Numbers and words are both needed if we are to understand the world" (Miles & Huberman, 1994, p.40).

Quantitatively the study examined the level of teacher self-efficacy and its influences. To acquire more in-depth information of these influences and teachers' perceptions, open-ended, semi-structured interviews were carried out. Qualitative research as defined by Denzin and Lincoln, "is multi-method in focus, involving an interpretive, naturalistic approach to its subject matter. This means that qualitative

62

researchers study things in their natural settings, attempting to make sense of or interpret phenomena in terms of the meanings people bring to them" (2005, p.2). Additionally, qualitative research builds a "complex, holistic picture" (Creswell, 1998). Qualitative research allows the investigator to answer "how" and "why" questions and to compile a "detailed view" and narration of the research, as well as carry out the investigation in a natural setting (Creswell, 1998; Gay & Airasian, 2000).

This chapter describes the methodology and rationale behind the choice. It includes descriptions of the procedures.

Research Questions

Bandura (1977) stated that people's conceptions of their self-efficacy, whether accurate or misjudged, are developed through four sources of influence which he termed as (1) mastery experience or actual experience, (2) vicarious experience, (3) verbal or social persuasion, and (4) physiological arousal or emotional state. To examine the relevance of Bandura's model to the preparation of Montessori teachers, the following research questions were explored:

1. Do the independent variables of mastery experience, vicarious experience, verbal or social persuasion, and physiological arousal significantly predict self-efficacy among Montessori pre-service teachers?

2. How do pre-service teachers with high and low levels of self-efficacy explain the influences of mastery experience, vicarious experience, verbal or social persuasion, and physiological arousal on their level of teaching efficacy?

In addition, two secondary research questions were also examined:

3. What is the difference in scores on the Teachers' Sense of Efficacy Scale (TSES) between pre-service teachers and those that have completed their in-service?

4. Do the teachers with high levels of self-efficacy report different influences than teachers with low levels of self-efficacy?

Research Design

This study utilized a mixed methods design to investigate the relative strength of the sources in predicting teacher self-efficacy. The purpose of the quantitative phrase was to determine the level of teacher self-efficacy and to compare the average pre-TSES and post-TSES scores to see whether there was a gain. The influences on teacher self-efficacy were also examined to see which (if any) PIP dimensions predict efficacy accurately. Perceptions of Preparation (PIP) was a questionnaire prepared to better understand the influences (mastery, vicarious, verbal, and emotional) on a Montessori teacher's self-efficacy. In the qualitative phase, each of these influences was further explored through semi-structured interviews with the participants.

A quasi-random sample for the quantitative portion of the study and a purposeful sample for the qualitative portion of the study were utilized. The quantitative data was collected and analyzed first, followed by the qualitative data. The two sources of data

64

were then mixed at the interpretation phase of the research process. According to

Creswell and Plano Clark (2007), the design can also be classified as an Explanatory

design with follow up expectations. The study is attempting to explain the influences on

Montessori teacher self-efficacy quantitatively with a follow up qualitative portion that

attempted to support and expand upon the quantitative findings. The design is

demonstrated in Figure 3.7:

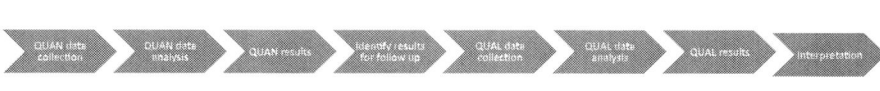

Figure 3.7: Explanatory design for self-efficacy study.

Since this mixed methods design is sequential, with the selection of participants

for interviews dependent on the quantitative analysis, I will describe the complete

methodology for the quantitative phase first, followed by the methodology of the

qualitative phase.

Quantitative Phase

Setting and Participants

       Quantitative data as described by Gay and Airasian (2000) "are used to describe current conditions, investigate relationships, and study cause-effect phenomena" (p, 11). Quantitatively this study examined efficacy in student engagement, instructional strategies and classroom management. It compared the average pre-training and post-training self-efficacy levels to see whether there was a gain. An additional questionnaire judged which influence was strongest on the teacher: mastery, vicarious, verbal, or physiological.

       The population of interest in this study was students that were admitted to Montessori teacher training programs throughout the United States. Only a small sample of the population was included in the study. To maintain consistency of study sites, the teacher training organizations chosen were accredited by Montessori Accreditation Council for Teacher Education (MACTE). MACTE is the international standard setting and accrediting body for Montessori teacher education and is recognized by the National Council for the Accreditation of Teacher Education (NCATE) and the Teacher Education Accreditation Council (TEAC).

       This study is not dependent on the age of the subjects. However, based on the average of traditional graduating college students and general retirement age, it is

66

estimated that subjects ranged in age from 23 to 65 years of age. Both males and females were included in the study and gender and ethnicity information was collected.

This study utilized a quasi-random design for the quantitative portion of the study and a purposeful sample for the qualitative portion of the study. Anticipating a 10 to 20% response rate, an email was sent to the Directors of all the Montessori teacher training programs in the USA enlisting their help. (Appendix A) The email explained the purpose and design of the research:

> *"As a part of my dissertation I am conducting research to gain a better understanding of the influences on self-efficacy for Montessori teachers. Teaching efficacy is an individual's perceived level of effectiveness for completing a teaching task. Clearly, an investigation into pre-service teacher self-efficacy and how these beliefs are conceived and nurtured can provide meaningful information to teacher educators and professionals responsible for designing and implementing more meaningful teacher preparation programs."*

The email included a letter to be distributed to all the students that explained the research as well as a consent letter for the participants. The consent form is provided in Appendix B. The letter incorporated a link to the survey that was set up on the internet survey provider Survey Monkey and an invitation to participate in the interview portion of the study. This is provided in Appendix C.

The reaction from the Directors of the teacher training programs was mixed. I received enthusiastic responses from some that supported research and were eager to participate. For example:

> *"First of all I would like to congratulate you on pursuing your studies and finding such a good topic for your research. Our teacher education classes start in September and I would be happy to relate your research to our students."* (Washington)

There were others that were glad to participate but were reluctant to give out any personal information (including email addresses) of their students and some that were concerned that their students would participate in the survey but would be reluctant to do the one hour interview. For example:

> *"......is not allowed to divulge names, addresses or email of our students. I am sorry we cannot comply."* (Texas)

There were a few training center that had several questions and really tried to make it work but:

> *"It looks like our students are not at the stage that fits your research situation and in the time frame that you need."* (New York)

Sadly I received many responses from teacher training organizations that were either shutting down or taking sabbaticals from offering their program. For example:

68

"Our program is about to close. We will not have any incoming students. Our last cohort of students will be completing their internship this coming school year and then our program will be closing." (Florida)

There were quite a few too that did not want to participate. This drastically cut down on the participants for the research. Students newly enrolled into Montessori teacher training programs were asked to take the TSES survey before they embarked on their training.[1] There were a total of 35 students that took the survey. Once they had completed their training, they were asked to take the survey again (TSES) along with an additional survey (PIP). This time demographic information was collected. There were 22 students, all female; who took the survey. Their ethnic distribution is as follows: Caucasian 15 (68%), Hispanic 3 (14%), Asian 2 (9%) and Other 2 (9%).

Each participant was also asked if they would consent to an interview at a later time, and if they agreed, they were asked to provide their name and phone number. Of the 22 students, 16 agreed to be contacted at a later date and gave their name and phone number.

Measures

Bandura's Socio-cognitive Theory of Self-Efficacy (1986, 1997) and the link of teachers' self-efficacy to student achievement provide the framework for the

---

[1] Permission to use the Teacher's Sense of Efficacy Scale (TSES) in this study was granted by Anita Woolfolk Hoy.

investigation (Bandura, 1997; Hoy, 2000). In this study, I explored the relationship between the independent variables of mastery experience, vicarious experience, verbal or social persuasion and physiological arousal or emotional state on a Montessori teacher's sense of self-efficacy. These variables were chosen in order to attempt to quantify the influences on teaching efficacy. These quantified relationships were compared to the relationships reported during the personal interviews. In order to form a complete picture of the impact on personal teaching efficacy (self-efficacy), it was advantageous to investigate beyond quantitative measures and employ qualitative methodology that provided teachers the opportunity to narrate and describe the influences on them and how they were affected (either positively or negatively). The hypothesis was that these independent variables, taken together, would account for significant variance in the dependent variable of teacher efficacy.

The dependent variable, which made up the first part of the questionnaire, was the long version of the Teachers' Sense of Efficacy Scale (TSES) (Woolfolk Hoy, 2001). This questionnaire is presented in Appendix D. According to Albert Bandura, motivation comes from people's judgments of their ability to carry out specific action and the anticipated consequences of those actions. Bandura identifies these concepts as efficacy expectations and outcome expectancies (1977). From these concepts, Gibson and Dembo (1984) developed a 30-item survey/questionnaire to correspond with Bandura's theory of self-efficacy and to measure efficacy as it is aligned with efficacy expectations and outcome expectancies. Hoy and Woolfolk went on to modify the Gibson and Dembo (1984) instrument. Hoy and Woolfolk (1993) found the first dimension of efficacy to "reflect a general belief about the power of teaching to reach difficult children … and (teachers') attitudes toward education" (p. 357), labeling this dimension as general efficacy. The second dimension reflected the "teacher's personal sense of efficacy" (p. 357) and was labeled personal teaching efficacy. From these two dimensions, a long 24-item version and a short 12-item version survey/questionnaire was developed.

The TSES long form asks for a self-report of teacher beliefs and was constructed using a nine-point, Likert-type response scale with the options of *1 (nothing), 3 (very little), 5 (some influence), 7 (quite a bit), and 9 (a great deal)*. The sentences on the scale all begin with the stems, "How much…," "How well…" or "To what extent..." and ask participants to gauge their abilities to handle various situations related to teaching. Participants are asked about their proficiency with instructional practices, maintaining classroom environments, and engaging students.

Three factors have been identified in both versions with loadings from .44 to .79: efficacy for instructional strategies, efficacy for classroom management, and efficacy for student engagement. For the purposes of this study, the 24-item version was used. The overall reliability and validity of the composite scale is .94. The authors of this study, Tschannen-Moran and Hoy note that "With pre-service teachers we recommend that the full 24-item scale be used, because the factor structure often is less distinct for these respondents" (2001). This version reported reliabilities of .87 for engagement, .91 for instruction, and .90 for management. Validity was determined when Gibson and Dembo (1984) performed a "multitrait-multimethod analysis that supported both convergent and

71

discriminant validity of the scale" (Hoy & Woolfolk, 1990, p. 289). For this study, the eight items that were summed to create the engagement scale were assessed to determine whether or not they formed a reliable scale using Cronbach's alpha. The alpha for the eight items was .92, which indicated that the items form a scale that has very high internal consistency reliability. The alpha for the instruction scale (.95) and the alpha for the management scale (.92) also showed very high internal consistency. In my analysis, only the combined score was used which was .93.

Four independent variables were employed, corresponding to the four ways in which Bandura argued that people develop a self of self-efficacy: mastery experience, vicarious experiences, verbal cues, and physiological cues. To measure these variables a new instrument, Perceptions of Participation, was developed for the purpose of this study. It underwent revision based on the empirical results to arrive at a set of questions that would have both logical construct validity (defined as fit with the definitions of Bandura's four constructs) and empirical construct validity, as demonstrated by exploratory factor analysis.

The variable of mastery experience was first operationalized in the study with the following questions on a five point Likert scale where 1 represents "strongly disagree" and 5 represents "strongly agree":

1. In my early experience of working with young children I generally felt successful.
2. I can recall experiences I have had working with difficult, unmotivated children, in which I successfully engaged them in productive activity.

72

3. Rate your satisfaction with your professional performance this year on a scale of 1 to 5.

4. I have had experiences presenting Montessori materials to children that have built my confidence as a teacher.

The variable of vicarious experience was operationalized by the following sample questions:

5. I felt that my advisor/mentor was supportive during my internship and this helped my confidence.

6. In my preparation I was able to observe truly skilled teachers.

7. My advisor/mentor played a positive role in my development as a teacher.

8. Rate the interpersonal support provided by your colleagues at your school this year on a scale of 1 to 5 (5=Very Good).

The variable of verbal or social persuasion was operationalized in the study by the following questions:

9. People I respect have told me I will be a good teacher.

10. I have people I can rely on who express confidence in me as a teacher.

11. My instructors encouraged me in ways that built my confidence.

12. My advisor/mentor provided me with positive, constructive feedback which was very useful to me.

The variable of physiological arousal or emotional state was operationalized in the study by the following questions:

13. In the work I have done with children, I have had a feeling of well being.
14. I have been nervous and experienced physical symptoms of anxiety while working with children.
15. I try to talk and explain my stress in order to get feedback from my colleagues.
16. At times when a child is being disruptive and not listening to me, I experienced sweaty palms and/or increased heart beat.

This questionnaire also asked the participants for demographic information (gender, ethnicity, and a self rating of their level of understanding of the Montessori philosophy and methodology). These factors were selected for the purpose of the study because the researcher viewed them as empirically promising and theoretically interesting. The questionnaire is provided in Appendix E.

Procedures

The first step in this study was to determine the reliability and validity of the PIP scales. Using SPSS, factor analysis was conducted to determine how closely the items fit into the constructs they were designed to assess. As described above, the measure was designed to address four factors or components, and four components were identified in the exploratory factor analysis, as shown in the rotate component matrix in Table 3.1. In the table, items 1 through 4 were designed to load on a Mastery component associated

74

with Component 1, items 5 through 8 with a Vicarious component associated with

Component 2, items 9 through 12 with a Verbal or social persuasion component

associated with Component 3 and items 13 through 16 with a Physiological arousal or

emotional state component associated with Component 4.

Table 3.1: Rotated component matrix

Rotated Component Matrix

	Component			
	1	2	3	4
Q1			.700	-.340
Q2	.568			.679
Q3	.785			
Q4	.638	.404		-.280
Q5		.925		
Q6		.788		
Q7		.807		
Q8		.919		
Q9	.869			
Q10	.918			
Q11		.262	.827	
Q12		.414	.754	
Q13	.702		.294	
Q14			-.832	
Q15	-.346	.496		.503
Q16	-.342	-.251		.787

Extraction Method: Principal
Component Analysis.

Rotation Method: Varimax with
Kaiser Normalization.

Items Measuring Mastery

Items 2, 3 and 4 of the PIP survey (see above) fit well with measuring mastery. Item 1 did not fit well with items 2, 3 and 4 and item 4 also fit with Vicarious. Therefore items 1 and 4 were dropped.

Items Measuring Vicarious

Items 5, 6, 7 and 8 of the PIP survey had high loadings and fit together well. So those were maintained on the scale.

Items Measuring Verbal or Social Persuasion

Items 11 and 12 of the PIP survey had high loadings and went well together. So did items 9 and 10 and they fit together well but not on that construct and hence they were dropped.

Items Measuring Physiological Arousal or Emotional State

Items 15 and 16 of the PIP survey went together well on that construct. Item 14 did not fit with 15 and 16 and so it was dropped.

Table 3.2: Second factor analysis results

Rotated Component Matrix[a]				
	Component			
	1	2	3	4
Q2				.932
Q3			-.749	.455
Q5	.938			
Q6	.776	.296		
Q7	.779	.358		
Q8	.922			
Q11		.949		
Q12	.326	.876		
Q15	.448		.670	
Q16	-.301		.826	.272

Extraction Method: Principal
Component Analysis.

Rotation Method: Varimax with
Kaiser Normalization.
a. Rotation converged in 5 iterations.

This is the second factor analysis, after omitting items 1, 4, 9, 10 and 14. The analysis supports the 4 dimensions. The only irregularity is item 3, which measures both emotional and mastery experiences.

Next, the internal consistency reliability of each of the revised PIP scales was determined. This is shown in Table 3.3.

Table 3.3: Internal consistency reliability of PIP scale

Independent Variable	Cronbach's Alpha	N of items
Mastery	.429	2
Vicarious	.902	4
Verbal	.882	2
Emotional	.460	2

The reliability Cronbachs alpha for Mastery was .429 which was very low. This construct was difficult to measure. The reliability Cronbach's alpha for vicarious was .902. This construct had very high reliability. The reliability Cronbach's alpha for verbal was .882. This construct had very high reliability. The reliability Cronbach's alpha for emotional was .460. This construct had low reliability.

Analysis

There were two stages to the analysis: comparing the pre and post results of the TSES, and using multiple regressions to address Research Question 1. The results of that analysis are presented in Chapter 4. The independent variables mastery experience; vicarious experience; verbal or social persuasion and physiological arousal or emotional state were chosen in order to attempt to quantify the influences on teacher self-efficacy. These quantified relationships were compared to the relationships reported during the personal interviews.

Qualitative Phase

Setting and Participants

After statistical analysis was completed, participants were identified. Since the standard deviation criterion was not possible (since there were not enough participants with extreme scores), I selected the four highest and four lowest scoring participants. There were 4 people in the high efficacy group and 4 people in the low efficacy group (Table 3.3). From these identified participants, eight people from each group had agreed in advance to participate in the interview portion of the study. Thus, a purposeful sample of four participants from each of these categories (Creswell, 1998; Morse, 1991) was selected and email queries were sent. All four of the high efficacy participants responded to the email query, while only three of the low efficacy participants responded. The remaining one identified low efficacy teacher was then invited to participate in the interview and s/he agreed. Thus, four people from the high efficacy group and four people from the low efficacy group completed the interview process.

Table 3.4: Mean scores.

Mean Scores (Pseudonyms used)

High Efficacy		Low Efficacy	
Jane	6	Jennifer	4.1
Lisa	5.71	Kathy	4
LeAnne	5.67	Carol	3.88
Torri	5.58	Maya	3.83

Mean of full set of TSES scores: 4.67

Standard Deviation of full set of TSES scores: 1.46

This analysis assumes that the high self-efficacy teachers are truly high, and low self-efficacy teachers are truly low, and that there is a reliable difference between them. Ideally, the high self-efficacy teachers should have TSES scores above 4.67 (mean) + 1.46 (standard deviation) = 6.13, and the low self-efficacy teachers should have TSES scores between 4.67 -1.46 = 3.21. In my study, none of the high self-efficacy teachers are that high, but there is still a full standard deviation difference between the lowest high self-efficacy teacher and the highest low self-efficacy teacher.

Data Collection

A semi-structured interview protocol was developed in order to guide the interview process and help the researcher gain a deeper understanding of the influences on Montessori teacher self-efficacy. The protocol is presented in Appendix G and the guiding questions are divided into four sections. Questions pertained to each of the independent variables and compared experiences of candidates whose efficacy declined or remained constant through the period of pre-service. The questions began with an attempt to put the candidate at ease:

1. Tell me about your Montessori training and elements of the course you enjoyed most.

2. Tell me about how you feel as a beginning Montessori teacher about to lead a class of children all by yourself?

This moved into questions that compared the influences on the teacher's self – efficacy:

3. Tell me about what you have read that has influenced your teaching. (Mastery)

4. Do you think your mentor /advisor had an impact on your confidence as a teacher? How? (Vicarious)

5. Sometimes families and friends of students are supportive and sometimes they are not. How supportive are your family and friends of you being a Montessori teacher? (Verbal)

6. How do you deal with your stress and anxiety? (Physiological)

Analysis

The qualitative data analysis began with a determination of the participants who scored higher than and lower than one standard deviation above the mean on the TSES. As described above, interviews were conducted with four participants from each group. The interview data was transcribed and the investigator read each transcript three times and then set it aside for several days to provide time for the investigator's reflection. This reflective process allowed time for the investigator to capture the subtle nuances of meaning and the insights of intuitive understanding (Denzin & Lincoln, 2005; Berg, 2004; Charmaz, 2006).

Analysis is an ongoing process that begins as soon as the data have been collected. I used an inductive process to search for possible meaning and discover patterns and connections that may exist among the interviews (Denzin & Lincoln, 2005; Berg, 2004; Charmaz, 2006). The transcriptions were read a fourth time to discern patterns, themes or concepts, theoretical insights, and possibilities for an emerging model on the influences on self-efficacy (Denzin & Lincoln, 2005; Berg, 2004; Charmaz, 2006).

I used constant comparative analysis for my qualitative data analysis because I wanted to explore the general questions I posed using the entire dataset to identify underlying themes (Leech & Onwuegbuzie, 2007). This method of analysis is appropriate when the researcher is attempting to gain an overall understanding of the data and wishes

82

to develop a possible theme based on the data (Strauss & Corbin, 1998). The reason for identifying four high self-efficacy and four low self-efficacy participants was to try to discover how differences in their formative experiences led them to have high self-efficacy or low self-efficacy.

Formatting Data into Tables

Microsoft Word functions were used for analyzing the text. Miles and Huberman (1994) have made known that table structures are powerful tools for data analysis. Nancy R. LaPelle (2004) has shown how effective this can be "for coding and retrieving, semi-automated coding and inspection, creating hierarchies of code categories via indexing, global editing of theme codes, coding of "face-sheet" data, exploring relationships between face-sheet codes and conceptual codes, quantifying the frequency of code instances, and annotating text." I began with creating a four-column table, where each separate response of the participant was entered into a new row of the table. The interviewer questions were interspersed in bold in separate rows. Although the order of the columns is not significant, the first column was used for the categorical coding and the second column represents High or Low efficacy level of the participant. The actual utterances of the interviewer and the participant are in the column three. A chronological sequence number is entered in column four for each separate response of the participant: "this sequence number is important as it allows you to return to the original sequence of utterances should you ever sort the table based on other columns" (La Pelle, 2004). Table 3.4 shows this initial formatting into a table.

Table 3.5: Interview statements on teacher self-efficacy

Level 1	Level 2	Text	SEQ
	H	**Tell me about your Montessori training and elements of the course you enjoyed most. Probe: In what ways did the course impact you? Positively or negatively?**	1
	H	I love learning how little minds think. I feel this is something I missed out in my Bachelors. It was not covered there. I think the course has impacted me positively.	2
	H	I have tried to apply some of the philosophy in the public education classroom where I currently teach.	3
	H	It has forced me to think outside the box. It makes me consider development a lot more in my classroom – what children may or may not be ready for rather than what they will be tested in.	4

Coding

Once the transcription in the tabular format was completed, I began to work with the coding scheme. I used open coding as "part of the analysis that pertains specifically to the naming and categorization of phenomena through close examination of data" (Strauss & Corbin, 1990, p. 62). In preparation for the analysis, codes were created by reading several of the interviews and noting themes that seemed to reoccur or that had some significance to the study. According to Strauss & Corbin (1990), "during open coding the data are broken down into discrete parts, closely examined, compared for similarities and differences, and questions are asked about the phenomena as reflected in the data. Through this process, one's own and others' assumptions about phenomena are question or explored, leading to new discoveries" (p. 62).

The analysis began with examining the data line by line. I broke the participants'

answers into chunks. Most of the chunks were about one or two sentences long; some

longer sentences were divided into smaller chunks. I then assigned codes to the chunks

using a deductive process. I felt that assigning predetermined codes to the chunks might

cause me to hear what I wanted to hear instead of what was actually stated. I took the

main idea of the chunk in assigning a code to it and sometimes I took a key word. Table

3.6 shows a sample of statements and the codes assigned to them.

Table 3.6: Sample statements and codes assigned.

Level 1	Level 2	Text	SEQ
		Tell me about your Montessori training and elements of the course you enjoyed most. Probe: In what ways did the course impact you? Positively or negatively?	1
5		I love learning how little minds think. I feel this is something I missed out in my Bachelors. It was not covered there. I think the course has impacted me positively.	2
1		I have tried to apply some of the philosophy in the public education classroom where I currently teach.	3
5		It has forced me to think outside the box. It makes me consider development a lot more in my classroom – what children may or may not be ready for rather than what they will be tested in.	4

I started by coding experiences that the High group reported that could have

contributed to their strong efficacy and related those to the four Bandura constructs

represented in the PIP instrument. I repeated the process with the Low group. Besides the

categories of Bandura's influences on teacher self-efficacy: mastery (1), vicarious (2),

verbal (3), and emotional (4), other codes included knowledge of theory (5), familiarity with materials (6), pacing of training(7), new and different (8), past success as a student(9.1), frustration as a student (9.2), perception of one's performance (10), attitude to children (11), ESL difficulties (12), and small class size (13). The codes were created by "reading a representative sample of interviews and noting the themes that seem to reoccur or that have some significance to the study" (LaPelle, 2004).

The initial process has "a priori" codes coming from Bandura's theory of self-efficacy (mastery, vicarious, verbal and emotional) plus emergent codes coming from the interview data. Once the codes were created, I began to fill in the code column (Level 1) in the tables. When all of the text in a row fell into one category that had been defined, one theme code was added to the table. For example in Table 3.7, the interviewer's question of the course's impact was answered clearly enough for the codes 13, 6, 8 and 1 to fit in.

Table 3.7: Coding

Level 1	Level 2	Text	SEQ
		Tell me about your Montessori training and elements of the course you enjoyed most. Probe: In what ways did the course impact you? Positively or negatively?	1
13		What I most enjoyed about my training was small class sizes; also the personal 1:1 ratio with the instructor for lessons and the questions about the lessons.	2
6		With this intimate setting I was able to practice the lessons several times and ask the questions I needed to. This made me really comfortable when I went into the classroom to give lessons to the students.	3
8		I also really enjoyed the cultural area of the philosophy. It went into real depth unlike other training centers where I don't think they go into such depth. I also enjoyed the Literacy area and the Pink, Blue, Green Series. I think that is a new and marvelous way to teach children how to read and write.	4
1		The course did impact me positively. Very much so. I feel like the course completely changed my life to be very honest. I had just come back from teaching in Ethiopia and I was lost. Did not know what I was going to do. I was teaching in a traditional classroom there and came here and taught in a Montessori classroom. And really felt it shifted my entire life. Not just my career path but my personal choices. Just sort of Montessori became engulfed in it – in every facet of my life. Even down to the cleanliness of my house!	5

Sorting Data Tables and Finding Patterns

Once the text was coded for themes, I moved onto the more complex analysis of searching and sorting the data for patterns. I started by comparing the experiences of Jane (the highest self-efficacy teacher) and Kathy (the lowest self-efficacy teacher). These two teachers are nearly two standard deviations apart in self-efficacy. I created a table (3.7) to

compare their experiences.

Table 3.8: High-low efficacy comparison

Group	Name	Main Explanatory Themes
H	Jane	School came easy to me. I did not really have to work hard to get those grades. So I guess my grades were my successes. (9.1) Technically I failed myself by not pushing myself harder but I did not fail anything. I could have done a lot better. It was not until I did my Masters' that I realized I had to work a lot harder than I had ever done before. (9.1)
H		
H		
H		
L	Kathy	Failures – I was not the best in academics and I wanted to be the best. This really bothered me as I tried so hard.(9.2)
L		
L		
L		

When this was completed and in a similar manner, I looked at the other

participants and added their responses (Table 3.9).

Table 3.9: Responses

Group	Name	Main Explanatory Themes
H	Jane	School came easy to me. I did not really have to work hard to get those grades. So I guess my grades were my successes. (9.1) Technically I failed myself by not pushing myself harder but I did not fail anything. I could have done a lot better. It was not until I did my Masters' that I realized I had to work a lot harder than I had ever done before. (9.1)
H	Lisa	Many of those! Successes – I was a very hard worker in school. Giving up was never an option. Even though I was in several special education classes, I still wanted to do my best. I worked very hard because I knew I wanted to go to college. I had fairly decent grades. (9.1) I had to learn that no matter how hard I worked A's were not going to happen. I had to learn that in most cases I was going to get a B or a C. I had to learn to compromise with that. It hurt my feelings a lot. I learned to become ok with it because I knew I was working to the best of my ability and I never gave up. (9.1)
H	LeAnne	Academically I was very good. I was good in all areas. I got good grades throughout. (9.1)
H	Torri	Successes –Varsity swim team and tennis. Lots of volunteer work. Went to a Catholic High School and there were always opportunities to do volunteer work. We went to shelters, etc. (9.2)
L	Kathy	Failures – I was not the best in academics and I wanted to be the best. This really bothered me as I tried so hard.(9.2)
L	Maya	I was very weak in anything to do with Math. Actually I did not pass any High School Math. But because I had so many credits, my grades were so high in other subjects, I passed with Honors. (9.2)

Table3.9 CON'T		
L	Carol	In high school there was a major event in my life. I studied in a Catholic school since Kindergarten in a small city in the mountains. I moved to a big city to go to school. It was a shock to me. I did not do well at all. My parents recognized it and moved me to a smaller school. I then did much better. That other school was all about grades and the emphasis was on passing for the exam. I just paralyzed. The other school had more of the social aspect although it was a Catholic school too. Spiritual education too–it was more in sync with what I had grown up with. I did very well once I changed the school. (9.2)
L	Jennifer	The successes were never very much encouraged. If we were doing something well it was kind of acknowledged but in a very neutral way. What was acknowledged was if you were not doing well. Parents were always encouraging but we had some very tough teachers. Especially in Latin our teachers were very tough. They used to tell us that if we were not good in Latin we would never be a support of society. And somewhere that struck a very deep chord. You try to shake it off but I have been carrying it for so long. The time we take in the morning when we reflect, I take the time to speak about what has been bothering me. I find myself shedding the whole skin. I feel like a fresh new baby.

The failure has helped me see what I don't want in life and the Montessori Method gives me such passion – it is such a positive way to teach the children. I do not want to treat the children the way I was treated. I don't think the teachers did it consciously but I do not want to teach that way. (9.2) |

Comparisons and Assertions

I then compared the coded themes of the high group and the low group to

determine how they were different. As the analysis proceeded, I searched for saturation

of repetitive patterns and the links between them (Denzin & Lincoln, 1994; Berg, 2004;

Charmaz, 2006). In order to maintain control over the data, I organized interview content

into separate files according to each code and theme. These files, organized around specific codes and themes, facilitated content analysis (Denzin & Lincoln, 1994; Berg, 2004; Charmaz, 2006). I was able to arrive at four assertions that summarized how the participants explained their own confidence or lack of confidence and what the systematic differences are between high TSES candidates and low TSES candidates.

Cross Method Analysis

The next chapter will elaborate upon the results of the data analysis methods presented in this chapter. It focuses on comparing the results of the two methods (qualitative and quantitative) employed. The two types of data are combined and analyzed to arrive at findings and conclusions with the aim being to show where these methods yielded similar or new information. The two approaches (statistical and interview-based) are examined to see if they gave a consistent explanation: for example, if the level of efficacy of the participants was best explained by previous experiences working with children that they interpreted as evidence that they had developed mastery of instructional techniques that equipped them to work successfully with hard-to-reach children or perhaps different explanations that ranged from perhaps the quantitative analysis emphasizing the importance of mastery experience but the interviews placing more importance on verbal feedback from mentors of supervisors. At the end of the chapter the information will be synthesized, tying together all of the data into an integrated whole.

CHAPTER 4

RESULTS

Introduction

The purpose of this mixed methods research study was to investigate the influences on self-efficacy for Montessori teachers. Quantitatively, the study examined the level of teacher self-efficacy and its influences. Each of these influences was further explored through qualitative semi-structured interviews with the participants from the quantitative pool. At the completions of the quantitative analysis, I identified individual participants who scored one standard deviation above and below the mean score on teacher efficacy. I then selected four high efficacy and four low efficacy interview participants. I structured the interviews in order to gain more information of each of the potential influences on teacher self-efficacy. The following research questions were explored:

1. Do the independent variables of mastery experience, vicarious experience, verbal or social persuasion, and physiological arousal significantly predict self- efficacy among Montessori pre-service teachers?

2. How do Montessori pre-service teachers with high and low levels of self-efficacy explain the influences of mastery experience, vicarious experience, verbal or social persuasion, and physiological arousal on their level of teaching efficacy?

In addition, several secondary research questions were also examined:

92

3. What is the difference in scores on the Teachers' Sense of Efficacy Scale (TSES) between pre-service and those that have completed their in-service?

4. Do the teachers with high levels of self-efficacy report different influences than teachers with low levels of self-efficacy?

This chapter first reports the results of the quantitative analyses, followed by the results of the qualitative analyses.

Quantitative Results

Research Question 1

In order to answer quantitative research question 1 (Do the independent variables of mastery experience, vicarious experience, verbal or social persuasion, and physiological arousal significantly predict self-efficacy among Montessori pre-service teachers?), I employed multiple regression, with the total TSES efficacy score serving as the dependent variable and the four PIP subscales serving as independent variables.

Model Summary

Taken together, the PIP variables were strongly predictive of efficacy. The model yielded a multiple correlation coefficient (R) of .838, an R square of .702, and an adjusted R square of .632 (p. <.001). Hence between 63% and 70% of the variance in efficacy can be predicted by the four PIP variables.

Of the four PIP variables, two predicted self-efficacy in significant ways, Mastery and Emotional (Table 4.10). The standardized beta coefficients suggest that Mastery predicts self-efficacy most (β = .695, p < .001) with Emotional associated with past experiences as the second best predictor of self-efficacy (β = -.367, p <.015). The coefficient for Emotional is negative because the scale assigns higher values to negative emotional experiences. Representative items include "I have been nervous and experience physical symptoms of anxiety while working with children" and "At times when a child was being disruptive and not listening to me, I experienced sweaty palms or increased heart beat" where 1 is "Strongly disagree" and 5 is "Strongly agree".

Table 4.10: Coefficients

Coefficients[a]

Model		Unstandardized Coefficients		Standardized Coefficients	T	Sig.
		B	Std. Error	Beta		
1	(Constant)	87.224	43.777		1.992	.063
	Mastery	18.243	3.657	.695	4.989	.000
	Vicarious	-1.485	1.862	-.117	-.797	.436
	Verbal	-.620	3.868	-.024	-.160	.875
	Emotional	-6.691	2.462	-.367	-2.718	.015

a. Dependent Variable: TSE2STotal

Research Question 3

In order to answer research question 3 (What is the difference in scores on the Teachers' Sense of Efficacy Scale (TSES) between pre-service and those that have completed their in-service?), I was not able to use a t-test for dependent variable to analyze the change in efficacy from pre to post because it is not possible to identify the individuals in order to match their pre and post scores. Consequently, I computed the mean and standard deviation of each administration of the TSES. These are reported in Table 4.11.

Table 4.11: TSES survey results

	Variance	n	Mean	Standard Deviation
TSES1	1345.00	33	157.94	36.67
TSES 2	1223.86	22	169.64	34.98

I used Cohen's *d* for the effect size measure of the change from pre to post (Table 4.12). Cohen's *d* is computed by dividing the mean difference between groups by the pooled standard deviation. The difference in means (169.64-157.94) was 11.7. I then divided this by the pooled standard deviation (36.01). The answer was .32. According to Jacob Cohen (1998) this would be a small to medium effect.

Table 4.12: Cohen's *d*

Cohen's *d*	Interpretation
0.2	Small
0.5	Medium
0.8	Large

This means that teachers that had completed their in-service reported a moderately higher level of self-efficacy.

Qualitative Results

In order to answer research Question 2 (How do Montessori pre-service teachers with high and low levels of self-efficacy explain the influences of mastery experiences, vicarious experience, verbal or social persuasion, and physiological arousal have affected their level of teaching efficacy?) and Question 4 (Do the teachers with high levels of self-efficacy report different influences than teachers with low levels of self-efficacy?), I conducted eight interviews exploring the influences on Montessori teacher self-efficacy. I asked four participants who scored high on teacher self-efficacy and four participants who scored low on teacher self-efficacy a variety of questions designed to examine possible efficacy influences. The interview protocol is presented in Appendix G. A portion of one high participant's response and one low participant's response to the question of how you feel as a beginning Montessori teacher about to lead a class of children all by yourself is presented in Table 4.13.

Table 4.13: Transcript of interview with one high and one low self-efficacy participant

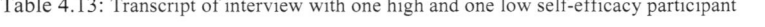

High Participant

I feel confident but also at the same time I am a bit nervous. Working with children and taking care of them is such a huge responsibility. I think the more you learn of Child Development and Montessori Philosophy the more you feel you do not know! I am constantly thinking of the children in my classroom and what lessons I should be giving them. It is always on my mind. I don't think ever stop thinking about the children and how best to meet their needs.

Low Participant

I am feeling more and more confident...I won't say I am ready totally...but I can see it every week more clearly...the possibility and the reality to be the lead teacher. We have been given the tools for it and I am slowly gaining in confidence. Of course I need a lot more practice with the materials and then working with the children.

Constant Comparative Analysis

In order to analyze the data produced from the eight interviews, I conducted constant comparative analysis on the low efficacy group and the high efficacy group. This method of analysis is appropriate when the researcher is attempting to gain an overall understanding of the data and wishes to develop a possible theme based on the data. The analysis begins with examining the data line by line. While this method is similar to Classical Content Analysis in the use of *in vivo* coding of each line, Constant Comparative Analysis has the researcher reusing *in vivo* or personal codes that apply to later text. The codes I used are presented in Table 4.14.

Table 4.14: Codes used for qualitative data analysis

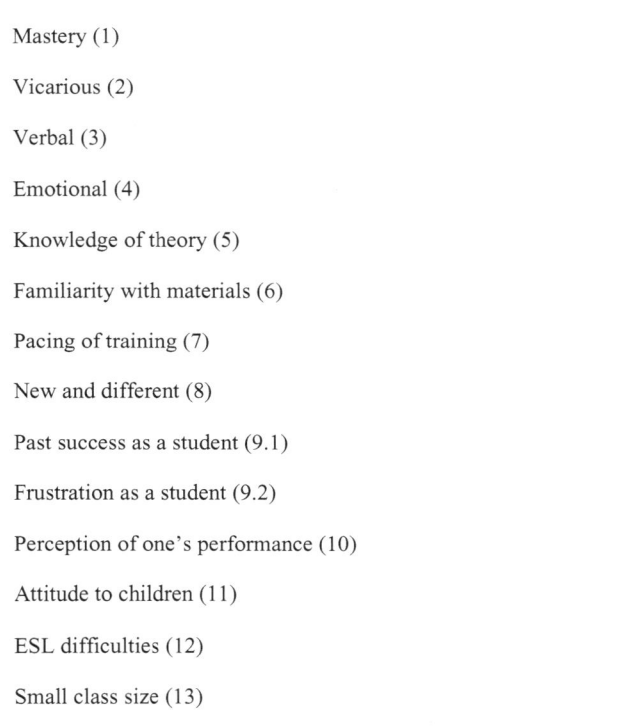

Mastery (1)

Vicarious (2)

Verbal (3)

Emotional (4)

Knowledge of theory (5)

Familiarity with materials (6)

Pacing of training (7)

New and different (8)

Past success as a student (9.1)

Frustration as a student (9.2)

Perception of one's performance (10)

Attitude to children (11)

ESL difficulties (12)

Small class size (13)

After all coding is completed; the researcher then searches the data for patterns with the intention of finding similarities or differences. I was able to arrive at five findings that summarized how the participants explained their own confidence or lack of confidence and what the systematic differences are between high TSES candidates and low TSES candidates.

Primary Findings

I will list each of the findings first and then describe how I arrived at them.

1. High self-efficacy teachers felt that high school was relatively easy and they faced fewer obstacles. On the other hand, low self-efficacy teachers felt that had many challenges.
2. All teachers showed a close relationship with their mentor.
3. The lead into Montessori for high self-efficacy teachers was directly targeted at them. For the low self-efficacy teachers the lead was a secondary influence.
4. Literacy in the Montessori curriculum resonated with the high self-efficacy teachers. Low self-efficacy teachers did not mention anything specific.
5. High self-efficacy students had teaching experiences in which they felt successful with difficult/challenging students.

Finding 1

The group of high self-efficacy teachers reported that high school was relatively easy for them and they faced few obstacles. They felt extremely proud of their achievements in high school and expressed confidence: "School came easy to me." and "Successes –many of those". On the other hand, the group of low self-efficacy teachers felt that had many challenges in high school. One of the teachers in this group spoke about her difficulties with Math and how she "was weak in anything to do with Math" and another expressed her frustration at not being good academically and how this really bothered her because she "tried so hard". The following quotes from the data support this theme:

Finding #	Group	Name	Quotes from interviews
1	High	Jane	School came easy to me. I did not really have to work hard to get those grades. So I guess my grades were my successes.
1	High	Lisa	Successes – many of those! I was a very hard worker in school. Giving up was never an option. Even though I was in several special education classes, I still wanted to do my best. I worked very hard because I knew I wanted to go to college. I had fairly decent grades.
1	High	LeAnne	Academically I was very good. I was good in all areas. I got good grades throughout.
1	High	Torri	Successes - Varsity swim team and tennis. Lots of volunteer work. Went to a Catholic High School and there were always opportunities to do volunteer work. We went to shelters, etc.
1	Low	Maya	Successes – well, I graduated with honors from High School. Very strong in English, journalism, year book, etc. These were important successes for me. But I was very weak in anything to do with Math. Actually I did not pass any High School Math. But because I had so many credits, my grades were so high in other subjects, I passed with Honors.
1	Low	Carol	In high school there was a major event in my life. I studied in a Catholic school since Kindergarten in a small city in the mountains. I moved to a big city to go to school. It was a shock to me. I did not do well at all. My parents recognized it and moved me to a smaller school. I then did much better. That other school was all about grades and the emphasis was on passing for the exam. I just paralyzed. The other school had more of the social aspect although it was a Catholic school too. Spiritual education too–it was more in sync with what I had grown up with. I did very well once I changed the school.
1	Low	Kathy	I was not the best in academics and I wanted to be the best. This really bothered me as I tried so hard.

1	Low	Jennifer	The successes were never very much encouraged. If we were doing something well it was kind of acknowledged but in a very neutral way. What was acknowledged was if you were not doing well. Parents were always encouraging but we had some very tough teachers. Especially in Latin our teachers were very tough. They used to tell us that if we were not good in Latin we would never be a support of society. And somewhere that struck a very deep chord. You try to shake it off but I have been carrying it for so long. The time we take in the morning when we reflect, I take the time to speak about what has been bothering me. I find myself shedding the whole skin. I feel like a fresh new baby.

This finding is important for educators because when students don't come to us with a general sense of efficacy based on their prior academic experiences, we need to pay attention to coaching them through experiences in order to prove that they are capable.

Finding 2

Both high and low self-efficacy teachers showed a close relationship with their mentor and had numerous positive experiences to share. They believed these experiences made a huge difference in their teaching by providing them with lessons, feedback and teaching examples. They were able to talk to their mentors and problem-solve specific issues. One teacher reported that they met once a week to go over lesson planning and the implementation of lessons. Another thought that she learned a great deal from just watching her mentor interact in the classroom. They all believed that this strong

102

relationship with their mentor impacted their confidence as a teacher. The following

quotes from the data support this theme:

Finding #	Group	Name	Quotes from interviews
2	High	Jane	My mentor has had a big impact on me as a teacher. She shows me everything and supports me. She makes me feel so confident. I love discussing Montessori with her! She is always encouraging and telling me I will make a good Montessori teacher. She provides me with positive feedback and that helps me a lot.
2	High	Lisa	We are very close and as the course progressed we have become closer and that always helps. Absolutely – she impacted my confidence as a teacher. Always showing faith in me as a teacher.
2	High	LeAnne	My mentor and I would meet at least once a week. But she was always there for me. She had a very good impact on me and helped my confidence grow. I knew she was always there. She would give me the whole class to handle. She would sit back and watch. This gave me a lot of confidence. Everything was an advantage of the mentor experience and I will keep in contact with her.
2	High	Torri	She was very supportive. She really allowed me to find that confidence. "You can do those math materials" she would tell me. "I know you know them." She helped me to study for the practical exams as well. Overall it has been very positive.
2	Low	Maya	Yes my mentor/advisor has had a big impact on me as a teacher. She has had an impact on me in the way that sometimes she knows better than me what I am ready for and encourages me to stretch myself. And is always respectful in guiding me. As opposed to making me feel that I don't know. Guiding me in a quiet way. In the way you would expect a good teacher to guide a child. To give me confidence. She encourages in me to find my own creativity. Was able to tap into my own reserves as a result of watching her. In other words I was inspired to reach deeper into myself as I watched her.
2	Low	Carol	She is very awesome. She has a lot of experience. She impacted me positively in my confidence as a teacher.

| 2 | Low | Kathy | She helped me a lot. She was very direct and that helped me a lot. She was never afraid to tell me when I was doing something wrong or was not good or if I had to change something. That was very helpful. |
| 2 | Low | Jennifer | Yes, my mentor had an impact on my confidence. We always have great discussions. When I talk with her, I find this passion coming up. She understands where I am coming from and she is able to appreciate that I have understood. Of course I will keep in contact with her. |

This finding is important for educators as it draws attention to the importance of mentoring relationships for interns. An intern becomes aware of his/her potential areas of growth through supervision and feedback. Positive feedback will enhance a positive attitude in the student and constant supervision will lead to the growth of specific traits and effectiveness as a teacher. It is also important that the supervisor model the traits of an effective teacher. Hence the way in which an internship is managed will have an influence on the development of a self-efficacious teacher. The value of a good mentor is immeasurable as both the high and low self-efficacy teachers in this study have attributed their confidence to their mentor teacher as the greatest influence on their development from intern to teaching professional.

Finding 3

The lead into Montessori for high self-efficacy teachers was directly targeted at them. A college teacher affirmed strongly, "Absolutely. That is the way to go." And this external influence impacted the teacher by giving her the confidence that she was going to be good at this. It made her go into the program better prepared and she was ready to live up to someone else's expectations of her. For the low self-efficacy students the entry

into Montessori was a secondary influence and mostly self-initiated. They did not have

the strong external influence that made up for the very positive attitude of the high self-

efficacy teachers. The following quotes from the data support this theme:

Finding #	Group	Name	Quotes from interviews
3	High	Jane	My son. When I put him in a Montessori school, I saw the differences in him. I watched him and how fast he grew overnight. His teacher is amazing and her excitement as she tells me what he is doing. The excitement of the teachers and how they love their jobs makes me feel that I want to work there. The teachers in the school said this would come naturally to me and that I was ready for the training.
3	High	Lisa	I think my teacher in College. He brought up Montessori in a child development class. We did a little research on it. I went in afterwards and asked him if he thought this was a good fit for me. And he looked me dead in the eyes and said "Absolutely. The right way to go." It was him to him I owe Montessori but a few other teachers to become a teacher.
3	High	LeAnne	I was looking for schools for my son and I heard about Montessori from my sister who thought it was a good for my son. When I was touring all the schools the philosophy of Montessori really struck out to me. It was different. I thought this was a good fit for me and I was ready to try it out.
3	High	Torri	My mentor. She has been teaching Montessori for 26 years. When I went into her classroom as an assistant I did not understand what she was doing necessarily but I thought it was amazing. I saw it was working but I did not know what she was doing. That was my first introduction to spurring my interest.

3	Low	Maya	Myself. When I started working in a Montessori classroom as an assistant. I was working under a teacher who was about 22 years old. She had got an online Montessori certificate. Occasionally in team meetings, I would ask questions or make a comment. I would be told or I would over hear others saying about me, "don't ask her she is not certified". I was offended that I was not respected for my knowledge. I realized I did not know Montessori. Then I started researching classes and courses. It was really just me. And you know after a couple of months the administration wanted me to take classes. They may have seen that I had it in me to be a good teacher. But I always felt that they thought I never measured up. So it was always me. I felt like I had to prove myself.
3	Low	Carol	This person I knew influenced me to become a Montessori teacher. I could not believe the daycare my son was at. I started to question a lot of things. Why he had to be in a bouncy chair all day when he could walk. He would cry and cry and no one would pick him up. I decided to do some research and came across Montessori. I then found an infant community in a home. When I stepped into this house, I was totally amazed. It was a prepared environment for this age group. The teacher was very well trained and was very passionate. She just inspired me and I thought I could do this. I looked around for training and that is how I came to it.
3	Low	Kathy	When I came to the USA, I was a nanny. The children went to a Montessori school. I liked how they did things and how they learned. They were very bright kids. I wanted to know why they were like that. How the school was like. I was curious how they learned. Then I started to read about it and that introduced me to Montessori.
3	Low	Jennifer	Probably the tough time I had in my own school. I needed the life experiences I have to fully give the child what I think the child deserves and needs to have. I hope that my experiences can help the child and that is why I chose to be trained as a Montessori teacher.

This finding is important for educators as it draws attention to the fact that students come to Montessori training from all walks of life and with all sorts of experiences behind them. Some have thought about the training for a while and others might not have put a lot of thought into it. It is important to know the background of the students and what brought them to Montessori. During the enrollment interview it is best to find out how serious the student is and if this is something they really want to do or it is a passing fancy. If it is the latter than it is best to show them that they belong here and that this is a niche for them. They will require a lot of encouragement and it will be necessary to keep them motivated by giving them more frequent feedback and building up their confidence.

Finding 4

Literacy in the Montessori curriculum resonated with the high self-efficacy teachers. Of all the curriculum areas in a Montessori classroom, literacy is the one area that all students can relate to. We have all learned to read and write and we all have an opinion on how good or bad the reading and writing scheme was. This helps us relate to this area by showing us how similar it is in its objectives and yet how different can be the way in which the objectives are met. Other areas are very Montessori based but literacy strikes a balance between conforming to the traditional model and arriving at it in a totally different, more effective way. Hence the difference is more tangible. Moreover the efficiency of the area in how the children learn and excel is obviously clear to them – "I worked so hard with him. Today he is reading and journal writing." The low self-efficacy teachers did not mention anything specific that resonated with them in the Montessori

curriculum. The following quotes from the data support this theme:

Finding #	Group	Name	Quotes from interviews
4	H	Jane	I lack knowledge in science and social studies because I have not really taught them in the public schools where I currently work. But I love those subjects and if I had to teach them, it would come easy to me. I could easily learn about them and then teach them. Right now I teach reading, writing and math only.
4	H	Lisa	I got into Montessori in College and now have found that I really enjoy it and it is a place for me to become a teacher. I have enjoyed a lot of the subjects of Montessori. So far my favorite is Literacy. Coming from a background of learning to read using phonics, it makes so much sense to introduce it at such a young age. Literacy area. Getting to know the materials better and the lessons that go with it has made me more confident. Literacy – because of past learning has been difficult for me. I was worried about the area. I have dyslexia. Didn't start reading until very late and I am not a strong reader. So teaching someone else to read makes me very nervous. Learning a different method to teach the children has led to my confidence.
4	H	LeAnne	One of my Pre-K children who did not know even one sound when I began teaching in his class. To begin with he would not even come near me. He would not listen to me. He would walk away from me. I worked so hard with him. Today he is reading and journal writing. In Math too he is doing well. It is beautiful to see now. I am happy. I am thankful.

4	H	Torri	I also really enjoyed the cultural area of the philosophy. It went into real depth unlike other training centers where I don't think they go into such depth. I also enjoyed the Literacy area and the Pink, Blue, Green Series. I think that is a new and marvelous way to teach children how to read and write.
4	Low	Maya	Well, I felt very successful when I had a child read at the farm table. I have never had a child read with me. I was the happy recipient but it was really the child's doing.
4	Low	Carol	-
4	Low	Kathy	-
4	Low	Jennifer	-

This finding is important for educators because it shows the importance when students are struggling and lacking in confidence to take them into familiar territory and helping them to see the effectiveness of the Montessori teaching tools. If the teacher has an opportunity to practice with the materials and actually work with the children her/his confidence will increase. This is true of the low self-efficacy teacher who expressed how successful she felt when she "had a child read at the farm table. I have never had a child read with me."

Finding 5

The teachers from the high self-efficacy group shared teaching experiences in which they felt successful with difficult/challenging students. These experiences have had many benefits to teacher self-efficacy. They believe they have become stronger teachers because of it and report having additional teaching skills; more knowledge of different teaching methods and a greater ability to diagnose student problems. A resilient sense of efficacy develops as a result of overcoming obstacles through perseverant effort and sustaining effort no matter what the setbacks and difficulties are. This was by far the strongest difference between the high and low self-efficacy teachers. The low self-efficacy teachers revealed the belief that they are becoming more confident and comfortable with their new roles as Montessori teachers but lack much teaching experience. The one teacher in the low self-efficacy group that has had more experience showed a confidence that none of the others in her group had. All the teachers in this group revealed a sense of intimidation but their expectations for themselves included an increase in efficacy and confidence along with better familiarity with the Montessori teaching apparatus. The following quotes from the data support this theme:

Finding #	Group	Name	Quotes from interviews
5	High	Jane	I do not deal with stress very well. I do yoga almost daily. I think yoga is a way of life and is a mental thing not just a physical thing. I do not deal with stress very well and that is why I am changing my career. With NCLB it just gets worse every year. They are just numbers on a piece of paper and their feelings and abilities are not taken into consideration. This year at this school was the worst. Never before have I not had a Principal not like me. I moved from Arizona and after 14 years of teaching in public schools I felt as though this was my first year! I was making a lot of mistakes with the technology. There was not much training. Nobody was helpful. The beginning of this year was really tough and I felt like the worst teacher on the face of the planet. My main goal is to get them to believe in themselves and I think I can do this. I have one student who in the beginning of the year wanted to quit. She is in 6th grade and she was not doing anything. I spoke to her and asked her what she was doing. She said she wanted to quit school. So I gave her the rough talk. I told her not to

5			wait around for a guy to take care of her for good guys did not want uneducated girls. Later in class she yelled at me and said I do not want anger management. I told her I was not a counselor but just her teacher and I was trying to help her. That was it. She totally switched and she is now a star student. Her spelling has improved. She is trying so hard. It makes it all worthwhile. She is the one I remember most and I know I can do the same with other children.
5	High	Lisa	I do babysitting as well and some of the activities we have learned in school has helped a lot with the sometimes difficult kids.

It takes a lot of practice to know them (Montessori materials) and with that knowledge I will be able to reach out to the most difficult students.

I worked with a child that was not engaging in any activity on Pink Box 1. I went all the way through and felt she understood what we were doing and wanted to do it on her own. That made me feel really good and confident. |
| 5 | High | LeAnne | Fairly confident. I think I have achieved quite a lot already...I have shown some progress in the school I am working in. I had some challenging kids and I was able to work with them fairly well.

My director said I am doing well with them. We have kids with ADHD, dyslexia, etc and I am doing my best to work with them and get the best out of them. The parents are very happy too.

This kid has all kinds of issues – sensory integration, dyslexia, ADHD. I would work with him well over the week and he would make some progress. Then the weekend would come and on Monday we would have to start all over again. This was so discouraging and disheartening for me but I never gave up. |
| 5 | High | Torri | Yes. I have a child in our classroom, that has behavioral issues and I did not know how to deal with it. I feel like I should have maybe done some more research. I feel like I could have taken a few more steps back. Even now I have some children that |

			definitely have some deviations that I need to take a step back and find out how to help them. Am I meeting their needs? What are their needs? What should I be doing?
			I am learning new things all the time – not only from others but also from bumps in the road that I face. I am always thinking a lesson could have gone better – I could have prepared the lesson better – understanding and getting to know the children and their needs makes me look at the materials from a different perspective. But it is a lifetime of learning.
5	Low	Maya	I am only now beginning to understand the children and their capabilities. I can see now how much they can be. I feel like I am learning along with them.
5	Low	Carol	My confidence has increased in all areas. I started new. I was not a traditional teacher. I had not worked with children before. There is nothing I had to unlearn and learn again.
5	Low	Kathy	I think well. I feel good because it is not like teaching them the areas but following them. You can change the presentation to suit the needs of the child. If one kid needs more interaction and the other kid needs something else, we need to change the method of teaching them. I feel good because I think I can find a way. I have had the opportunity of teaching lots of kids and I had good feedback from them.
5	Low	Jennifer	Of course I need a lot more practice with the materials and then working with the children.

Montessori teachers with high self-efficacy explain the influence of mastery experience as having most affected their level of teaching efficacy. They have had a lot more experience working with children than teachers with low self-efficacy. They have handled difficult children and view challenging situations as tasks to be mastered. They recover quickly from setbacks and disappointments as the teacher explained who worked hard with a child that "had all kinds of issues" over the week and then had to start all over again on Monday. She did not shy away from the situation but rather took upon herself a problem that had to be worked upon. Her success in the past with this situation gave her the confidence in her personal abilities. It impacted the way she set goals and tasks for herself and how she felt she could succeed in the situation.

Qualitative and Quantitative Results

The results of this study (both qualitative and quantitative) indicate that Montessori teachers with high levels of self-efficacy exhibit strong mastery experiences that account for the way they feel, and the goals they want to accomplish. This is consistent with the quantitative portion of the study as well as the qualitative which goes beyond what emerged in the quantitative analysis by validating the importance of mastery experiences to develop a strong sense of self-efficacy.

The quantitative results showed Emotional state (Bandura, 1998) associated with past experiences as the second best predictor of self-efficacy. However, the interviews with the participants did not provide further insight into the quantitative finding.

CHAPTER 5

DISCUSSION

Introduction

The purpose of the present study is to gain a better understanding of the influences on a Montessori teacher's level of self-efficacy. Specifically, I am interested in how we can prepare guides/teachers that believe in themselves and their ability to handle the children when they enter the classroom. Since developing efficacy in teachers that lack confidence in themselves is quite challenging, it is important to see how we can break down these barriers during the training itself (Labone, 2004). This is what drew my attention to this topic of research.

The research questions guiding this study depend on identifying specific efficacy influences, and on exploring the differences between high and low-efficacy participants. The research design was chosen in order to predict the influences, add to the current knowledge base, and to impact teacher education and professional development programs. The leading objectives of this mixed methods inquiry were to (a) build a statistical model that significantly predicts the influences on Montessori pre-service teachers' self-efficacy; (b) qualitatively examine the influences on Montessori teacher efficacy; and (c) gain a better understanding of the multiple influences on students who exhibit high and low self-efficacy. This chapter explores the results of the study through four main sections: (a) the outcomes of the study in relation to existing literature; (b) the implications of the findings; (c) the limitations of the study; and (d) suggestions for additional research.

114

Interpretation of Findings

In this section, I will explore the quantitative and qualitative study results of the main influences on teacher self-efficacy, and the important differences between high and low-efficacy Montessori teachers. Albert Bandura claimed learning environments conducive to students' achievements are created by a teacher's talent and by her belief in her ability to impact the learning experience, known as "teacher self-efficacy" (Bandura, 1997). Bandura's self-efficacy influences of mastery (content knowledge and previous teaching experience); vicarious experience (or mentor support); verbal persuasion (or encouragement from colleagues and comparable others); and physiological arousal (or internal sources such as anxiety and stress) each contributed to overall self-efficacy levels, but the findings of this study indicate that mastery is the best predicator of efficacy. According to the study, physiological arousal is the next best predicator of efficacy. The findings also show that there are three direct influences on Montessori teacher self-efficacy: knowledge of theory; classroom experience; and mentor support. A reconstructed conceptual framework depicting the direct influences on Montessori teacher self-efficacy is presented in Figure 5.5.

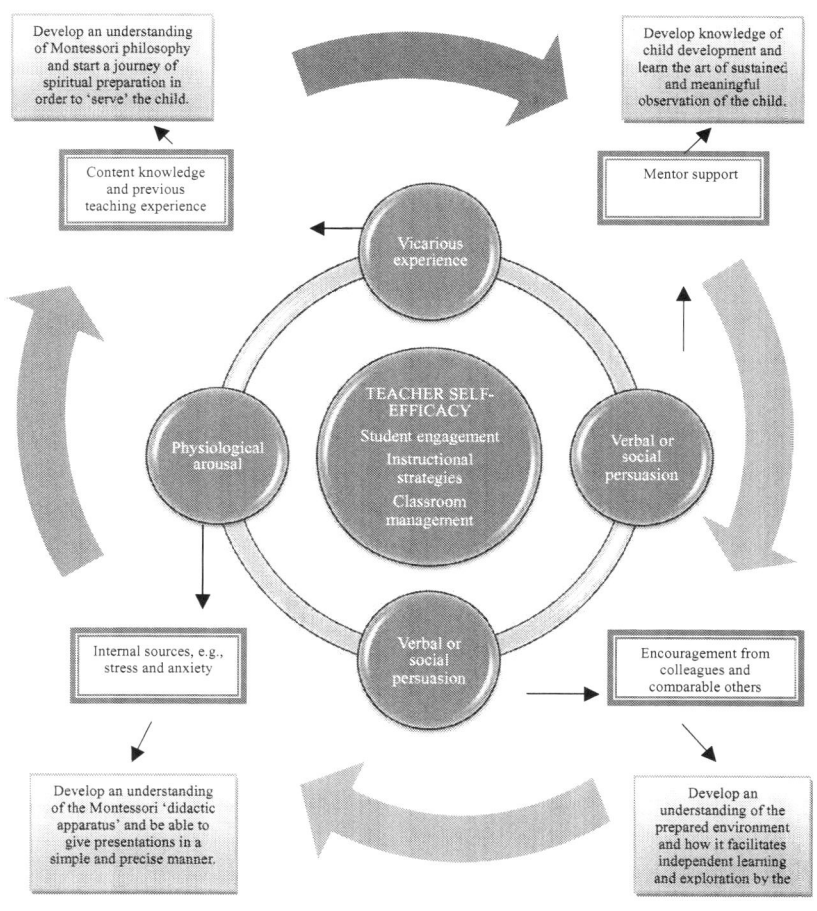

Figure 5.5: Reconstructed conceptual framework

This diagram connects Bandura's four sources of teacher self-efficacy with matters of importance to the teachers introduced during their interviews. Although, these do not quite fit into one of Bandura's categories, they do give insights into processes associated with teacher preparation and with what contributed to their efficacy levels. The first source, mastery experience, refers to the interpretations individuals make of their past performances. According to Bandura, "the most effective way of developing a strong sense of efficacy is through mastery experiences" (1995, p.3). Performing a task successfully strengthens an individual's sense of self-efficacy; however, failing to adequately deal with a task or challenge can undermine and weaken that sense. The best mastery experiences should take time and effort to accomplish. People who experience only quick and easy successes may actually be hurting themselves. If a more challenging task arises, it may cause the person to become frustrated and stressed, thereby decreasing his or her self- efficacy.

Bandura's hypothesis that interpretations of past performance serve as a strong indicator of self-efficacy was confirmed in studies on the sources of student self-efficacy (Usher & Pajares, 2008). When students can actually see themselves coping effectively with difficult situations, their sense of mastery is heightened. As one of the high self-efficacy teachers indicated in her interview in this study, "I am fairly confident. I think I have achieved quite a lot already…I have shown some progress in the school I am working in. I had some challenging kids and I was able to work with them fairly well." She credited her training for her confidence: "The curriculum plus the one year of internship has given me a lot of confidence. The curriculum covered 100 percent of

117

everything that is required in the school that I am teaching in." This study shows that knowledge of Montessori philosophy, methodology, and teaching experience gradually leads to higher self-efficacy. For example, a teacher favorably interprets being successful in helping a student increased her sense of self-efficacy. On the other hand, failures in the classroom lowered a teacher's belief in what she or he can do.

The second source, vicarious experience, refers to the experience gained by observing the successes and failures of others. As Bandura stated, "seeing people similar to oneself succeed by sustained effort raises observers' beliefs that they too possess the capabilities to master comparable activities required to succeed" (1995, p.3). Thus, according to Bandura, a person forms beliefs in his own efficacy when he watches someone similar model the desired behavior. For example, films and videotapes have been used successfully to encourage socially-withdrawn children to interact with other children. The child viewing the film sees a model child—someone much like himself—experience success and comes to believe that he can also do the same thing (Conger & Keane, 1981). Common examples of vicarious experiences enhancing self-efficacy include advertisements for weight-loss and smoking-cessation programs that feature testimonials from successful people. Teachers in this current study observed the performance of their colleagues to evaluate their relative capabilities and to draw confidence from that experience. In other words, they were able to identify closely with their mentor and their self-efficacy grew from observing and modeling her/him. Researchers suggest that beginning teachers with higher levels of induction support compared to those with lower levels of support are more likely to view their jobs as manageable; to report that they can teach the most difficult students; and to indicate that they are successful in providing education to special-needs students (Billingsley et. al., 2004).

The persuasive messages individuals receive from others (verbal or social persuasion) is the third source examined in this study. Bandura asserted that people could be persuaded to believe they have the skills and capabilities to succeed; positive messages typically boost self-efficacy, whereas negative appraisals tend to be discouraging. Bandura elaborated by determining "people who are persuaded verbally that they possess the capabilities to master given activities are likely to mobilize greater effort and sustain it than if they harbor self-doubts and dwell on personal deficiencies when problems arise" (1995, p. 4). This is likely why teachers who think they have very supportive principals are less stressed and are more committed to and satisfied with, their jobs as compared to those who perceive less support (Billingsley & Cross, 1992). In this study, encouragement from colleagues and peers modified how capable the new teachers felt in their jobs, which affected their perceptions of efficacy. This gradually led to a sense of confidence in being able to prepare an environment, self-assuredly understanding the needs of the children and meeting them with a classroom that facilitates independent learning and exploration by the child. Positive verbal messages can have a big impact here and are able to persuade the individual to put in that extra effort when faced with difficult tasks. As one of the high self-efficacy teachers's explained, "She [mentor] was very supportive. She really allowed me to find that confidence. 'You can do those math materials,' she would tell me. 'I know you know them.'"

The final source of self-efficacy, physiological and emotional states, refers to an individual's somatic and affective responses regarding their performance. Moods, emotional states, physical reactions, and stress levels can all impact how a person feels about their personal abilities in a particular situation; excessive stress or anxiety can convince a teacher she does not have the skills necessary to carry out her job successfully. For example, the multiple pressures on special education teachers pose legitimate concerns for increased stress, which has been associated with burnout and teacher attrition (Billingsley et. al., 2004; Boyer & Gillespie, 2000). According to Bandura, "it is not the sheer intensity of emotional and physical reactions that is important but rather how they are perceived and interpreted" (1995, p. 5). As seen in this research study, grasping Montessori's 'didactic apparatus' and being able to give presentations in a simple and precise manner reduces anxiety and improves the teacher's sense of self-efficacy, whereas struggling with the material presentations can have a negative impact on self-efficacy.

These sources are further explored under the following categories: acquiring knowledge of Montessori philosophy and methodology; classroom experience and familiarity with the material; and mentor support.

Acquiring Knowledge of Montessori Philosophy and Methodology

Maria Montessori's legacy is a materialized pedagogy in which educational knowledge is presented to children in multimodal form. Designed for use by children from birth to twelve years old, the objects manifest a curriculum that scaffolds incrementally and systematically across all the subject areas. Students training to be Montessori teachers receive knowledge of her philosophy and methodology through lectures, demonstrations, and practice sessions. On the basis of notes taken during the training sessions, students compile albums of Montessori theory, materials, and procedures. The albums become a component of the student's assessment and, ultimately, a resource from which their future practice is based. Other components of the assessment include essays and observations that display an understanding of Montessori principles and, most importantly, an extended oral and written examination that asks students to demonstrate any of the materials from memory in order to display their mastery of the pedagogy.

To prepare teachers for the challenging role she outlined for them, Montessori devised a thorough training course based on a deep understanding of content knowledge that catered to the students' thinking. As Montessori aptly noted, "when adults provide clear limits but set children free within those boundaries, and sensitively respond to children's needs while maintaining high expectations, children show high levels of maturity, achievement, empathy, and other desirable characteristics (Lillard, 2005, p. 32-33)." This study clarifies that knowledge of Montessori theory and materials leads to mastery experiences. Some teachers with unusually high levels of efficacy spoke about content knowledge as contributing to their confidence. As one of the high-efficacy teachers in this study said, "I really feel the lectures on child development helped a lot which is why I say I would not change the exams because it taught me a lot. I can now see it in practicality in the classroom—why things are happening." Their knowledge of child development theories and ability to deal with children as effectively as possible contributed to their mastery experiences and a high level of self-efficacy. Researchers e found that pre-service teacher efficacy beliefs are enhanced by university courses that provide student teachers with hands-on activities, experience writing lesson plans, or opportunities to teach brief lessons (Cantrell, Young, & Moore, 2003; Watters & Ginns, 2000). The results of this study also indicate that some of the high self-efficacy teachers felt a strong need to keep learning and becoming experts in their field. As one of the teachers said, "I think the more you learn of Child Development and Montessori Philosophy the more you feel you do not know". On the other hand, the low self-efficacy teachers did not demonstrate any desire for additional learning opportunities.

Classroom Experience and Familiarity with the Materials

In this study, teacher self-efficacy increased through classroom experience. The high self-efficacy group, which acknowledged the effect of material proficiency on their level of confidence, had significantly more classroom experience than the low self-efficacy group. As a high efficacy teacher in this study explained, "I am getting familiar

122

with the Montessori materials. It takes a lot of practice to use them well and with that knowledge I will be able to reach out to the most difficult students."

Montessori developed a specific set of materials "carefully designed to confer specific understanding through repeated use and in the context of other materials, selected to avoid most redundancy, and quantified to allow mastery in about three years in the classroom" (Lillard, 2005, p 323). Unlike teacher-training programs that give trainees a theoretical orientation to their work, teacher training in Montessori is intensely practical. This is because the Montessori Method is primarily a hands-on approach to learning where the objects are designed to capture and to hold the attention of children. As a result, teacher trainees must spend a lot of time working with the materials and understanding them; in turn, the familiarity with the materials builds their confidence to give flawless presentations to the children. The completed albums of the teacher trainees, with lesson plans and diagrams, become a theory of practice that remains the groundwork of teaching throughout their careers. These albums, created during the academic portion of the course, become their source of information for the materials and their presentations during their career as a Montessori teacher.

The variations in Montessori teacher training programs themselves are immense, however. There is not one single way to implement the Montessori philosophy (Corry, 2006), and since the Montessori name is not trademarked (Ruenzel, 1997), it is impossible to fuse Montessori education together (Schapiro, 2003). Montessori purists who strictly follow Montessori's original philosophy are very critical of those who practice a more modern approach to the Method. Others claim the purists refuse to see the philosophy's potential and practice (Hainstock, 1997). This divide remains among Montessori schools today. As a result, any school could theoretically call themselves a Montessori school (Chattin-McNichols, 1992).

As mentioned earlier, the Montessori pedagogy is largely an oral tradition handed down from one generation to another; this has caused it to splinter into a wide array of organizations and centers worldwide. Consequently, Montessori diploma courses vary from country to country and from organization to organization. Courses run anywhere from three years, to a year, to six months' and some distance learning courses do not even require a practical workshop element. It is obvious there are differences in the amount and detail of lessons on the materials and the exercises, on the rigorousness of the training, and on the authenticity of the Montessori approach.

Practice sessions with the materials and classroom experience also contribute to teacher self-efficacy. This is crucial since many of the study's participants voiced practice sessions with the materials as a contributor to self-efficacy. As one student said, "With this intimate setting, I was able to practice the lessons several times and ask the questions I needed to. This made me really comfortable when I went into the classroom to give lessons to the students." Those with low self-efficacy also mentioned that unfamiliarity with the materials affected their ability to be a good teacher. Thus, it appears that training centers ought to emphasize practice with the teaching materials, knowing that familiarity with them will aid in higher self-efficacy levels—even if that increases the demands on the student teacher.

Mentor Support

The mentor plays a very important role during the internship/practicum phases of Montessori teacher training. With years of experience in the classroom, they are able to provide advice and support to the trainees, guiding them to reach their goals. The high and low self-efficacy teachers interviewed for this research all revealed how much they valued and appreciated the support of their mentor; this contributed to their vicarious experience. The teachers reported that their experiences with a mentor made a huge difference in their teaching by providing them with lessons, feedback, and examples; they appreciated being able to problem-solve specific issues with their mentors. As a high-efficacy teacher in this study said, "My mentor was always there for me. She had a very good impact on me and helped my confidence grow. I knew she was always there. She would give me the whole class to handle. She would sit back and watch. This gave me a lot of confidence."

The high and low self-efficacy teachers both believed that a very supportive mentor helped them to become better teachers. Several previous studies on teacher efficacy and mentor support have had similar results: Philippou and Charalambous (2005) determined that mentors could increase teacher efficacy through effective feedback that was supportive and constructive. Two other studies also emphasize the important role of the mentor by determining that mentor support and collaboration have a strong impact on teacher efficacy (Mulholland & Wallace, 2001 and Poulou, 2007).

The mentoring teacher is extremely important to Montessori teacher trainees, who come out of training with theoretical knowledge ready to be put into practice. From the mentoring teacher they learn classroom management skills, record keeping, and all the practical aspects of working with young children. This puts a lot of responsibility on the mentor, who must model carefully and guide in a very gentle manner. With the variety of Montessori teacher-training programs, there are differences in this area of the course as well. There are some teacher-training organizations that do not have an internship at all, and others that allow self-directed internships. It is abundantly clear from this research that the teacher trainees appreciated a good internship under a supportive mentor, which implies that the mentor should be properly trained.

Each of these teacher self-efficacy influences (knowledge of theory, classroom experience, familiarity with the materials, and mentor support) contributed to the overall efficacy levels.

Implications of the Findings

The results of this study underline the need for Montessori teacher education programs to improve the quality of their training in order to allow students to develop a high sense of self-efficacy. The development of self-efficacy is an essential first step toward becoming a successful Montessori teacher, as "the real preparation for education is the study of one's self. The training of the teacher who is to help life is something far more than the learning of ideas. It includes the training of character; it is a preparation of the spirit" (Montessori, 2007, p. 120). This inner preparation takes time and guidance. The preparation of a Montessori teacher involves slow, personal changes that come from being an astute observer, especially as it is not easy to "check those inner attitudes characteristic of adults that can hinder our understanding of a child" (Montessori, 1966, p. 153). Montessori envisioned the teacher observing the child much as a scientist observes an experiment; this primary function would allow the teacher to direct the child towards the activities and materials which help him mature along natural lines. Montessori believed that:

> The teacher must bring not only the capacity, but the desire to observe natural phenomena. In our system, she must become a passive, much more than an active, influence, and her passivity shall be composed of anxious scientific curiosity, and of absolute respect for the phenomenon which she wishes to observe. (Montessori, 1912, p. 87)

Adults, claimed Montessori, could understand the phenomenon of human development only by seeing the children in the classroom. Naturally, such a process takes time and guidance by experienced teachers; since teacher-training programs are now cutting corners, this new breed of teachers is ill-prepared to meet Montessori's desire for "scientific curiosity." As Angeline Stoll Lillard wrote:

> Many Montessori teacher training programs are very short, lasting only a few weeks or months. Some programs attempt to educate Montessori teachers largely through internships, yet they do not ensure that the supervising Montessori teachers meet any standard…Correspondence courses have also become common, with obvious potential problems. (Lillard, 2005, p. 329-330)

Learning to be a Montessori teacher involves knowledge of theory and

procedures for working with the materials, as well as forming connections between the

philosophy and the methodology. Accordingly, changing the Montessori education

system to give trainees time to accept a strong conceptual understanding of the

underlying concepts will help them to succeed in the classroom. Reflecting on the status

of Montessori teacher-training programs today, Aline Wolf posed a pertinent question:

> Today the curriculum and schedule of Montessori training centers is determined
> by time restraints, finances and practicality. What was once a two year training
> course is now finished in one year or is often reduced to several weeks in two
> consecutive summers with one or two days per month of classes during an
> internship in the intervening school year. In even more extreme cases training
> is limited to a correspondence course followed by two or three weeks of practical
> experiences with materials. Where is the time for the best preparation for teaching?
> (Wolf, 1996, p. 34)

This research study demonstrates that high self-efficacy teachers have more confidence in

their conceptual understanding of the philosophy and methodology, which gave them

additional assurance as Montessori teachers. We must strive to increase the self-efficacy

of all Montessori teachers so that our children will have the best possible start to

education.

The current study also suggests that teacher education institutions should establish

strong mentoring/coaching programs to provide teacher trainees with the necessary

support and guidance. Each candidate interviewed for this research study—regardless of

high or low self-efficacy—spoke of a close relationship with his mentor and how grateful

he was for this dialogue. Learning classroom management and teaching styles from a

mentor is important during an internship as "we must be willing to accept guidance if we wish to become effective teachers" (Montessori, 1966, p. 34). Standards for supervising teachers, based on years of classroom teaching and professional development along with school support, are imperative to selecting a good mentor. This should include an intern-mentor meeting every day to answer questions and to plan the following day. This is important to note because "good classroom teachers are usually too focused on the children during the school day to simultaneously explain to an intern the many variations and nuances of the materials (if they even learned about them in their own training), and at the end of the day might be too tired to do so" (Lillard, 2005, p. 329).

Studies of teacher efficacy show that one possible way to promote a more realistic sense of self-efficacy in pre-service teachers is to provide them with mastery experience in the form of observations and field placement. Teaching is "a profession that is best learned through carefully structured, intensively supervised field experiences within an integrated teacher education program" (Worthy & Patterson, 2001, p. 336). Internship experiences provided in field-based blocks of courses are essential components for rethinking curricular reform in effective teacher education programs (Fang & Ashely, 2004; Haverback & Parault, 2008; Linek et.al., 1999; Worthy & Patterson, 2001). Field experiences expose pre-service teachers to a variety of teaching situations and ways to cooperate and communicate, which are essential components in providing a balance between classroom demands and teacher philosophy (Linek et.al., 1999).

The results of this study extend the results of Bandura's (1997) previous research, in which the four experiential sources— performance accomplishments (mastery),

129

vicarious learning or modeling, emotional arousal (anxiety), and social persuasion and encouragement— were important to the initial development of self-efficacy expectations. This research highlights the importance of knowledge of theory, classroom experience, familiarity with the materials, and mentor support as potential sources of teaching efficacy.

Limitations of the Study

The present study is by no means exhaustive, and provides only an initial survey on Montessori teacher self-efficacy. The study has limitations which make it difficult to generalize the findings, the main of which is the sample used. Despite the fact that all MACTE (Montessori Accreditation Council of Teacher Education)- accredited institutions were contacted to take part in this survey (over 120), only ten responded positively and agreed to take part in the research. I intended to have at least 100 students from all over the country participate in the study; instead, we had 33 participants in the pre-test and 22 in the post-test. Many of the training centers did not grant permission to take the names and information of their students for privacy reasons, and so it was difficult to run a t-test and to expound on their individual growth. It would have been interesting to see how the students' attitudes and confidence changed during the course of their study. The small number of individuals that responded consequently resulted in a lack of more extreme examples of high and low-efficacy teachers for interviews. Moreover, the Montessori Method attracts a broad spectrum of qualifications and diversity of backgrounds in its teacher-training programs, which makes it difficult to generalize the survey. The discrepancy in education levels in particular plays such a large role in evaluating the self-efficacy of teachers.

Cultural perceptions are another limitation of this study. Since an individual's cultural environment shapes his norms, values, and ideas (Minggang & Yuan, 2004), his self-efficacy is also dependent on the way in which he interprets the world. Success, therefore, is measured differently by various demographics—as is expressing that success. Researchers conducting cross-cultural communication work consistently find a distinct difference between individualistic and collectivist cultures regarding self-efficacy. Those in individualistic cultures have higher levels of self-efficacy and those from collectivist cultures, such as Asian cultures, have lower self-efficacy levels (even though they are often more successful in academic pursuits than those in individualistic cultures) (Scholz et.al 2002). For many students from collectivist cultures, academic motivation is driven by a fear of failure and an intense desire to please their parents (Eaton & Dembo, 1997); one of the interviewees in this study expressed this sort of cultural conditioning by mentioning that "successes were never very much encouraged. If we were doing something well it was kind of acknowledged but in a very neutral way. What was acknowledged was if you were not doing well."

Similarly, success can mean different things to different people. Again, collectivist and individualistic societies play a part in defining success. Since collectivist cultures tend to have a more realistic view of their abilities than individualistic cultures, they also tend to have lower self-efficacy levels. When asked to speak about "some of your successes and failures as a student in high school" during the interview portion of this study, one of the high self-efficacy teachers mentioned making varsity swim team and tennis. Others focused more on grades: "I was not the best in academics and I wanted to be the best. This really bothered me as I tried so hard." Klassen (2004) explains that "realistic—as opposed to optimistic—efficacy beliefs do not necessarily predict poor performance for all cultural groups, as has been suggested by self-efficacy theory." Hence, these researchers suggest there might be a variation in self-efficacy because individualistic cultures are too optimistic in their notions of self-efficacy, while collectivist cultures are more realistic.

Self-efficacy is influenced by many factors; among the most important are parents, peers, and teachers (Bandura, 1994). Since these factors vary widely according to culture, self-efficacy also varies depending on the values upheld in a specific culture. Since not all participants were from the same background, it was important to consider culture during the interviews. Almost all the participants open to sharing their experiences candidly were high self-efficacy teachers, while those unwilling to speak about their difficulties and struggles were of low self-efficacy. Pointedly, nearly all the low self-efficacy teachers came from typically collectivist societies. The different cultures represented in this sample may inhibit how each respondent interpreted success, and it is thus important to account for that discrepancy.

Direction for Future Research

This study provides much to contemplate in terms of future research. With the growing number of studies that show self-efficacy is a powerful variable in instructional effectiveness, it is important to thoroughly investigate what impacts efficacy within the context of teacher training. The results of the current study reveal a new conceptual framework for Montessori teacher self-efficacy, which opens up countless possibilities for future research. Firstly, new studies should be conducted to confirm the efficiency of the proposed PIP scale; we must determine whether the scale holds true for all Montessori teachers throughout the world, and whether the model works for elementary-school Montessori teachers as well.

Secondly, studies that explore the relationship between an understanding of the Montessori philosophy and methodology and teacher self-efficacy would be beneficial. This is particularly pertinent in light of the fact that the self-examination process is inherent to Montessori teacher preparation. Does high self-efficacy raise self-awareness or reduce it? This would be especially relevant as a longitudinal study that tracks low-efficacy teachers as they work to acquire a deeper conceptual understanding. In a similar vein, research focusing on how to structure professional development programs to enhance self-efficacy could be helpful to the teacher-training community.

A mixed-method study of a Montessori teacher trainer's perceived self-efficacy and its impact on the teacher trainees would also provide data for understanding this very complex topic. Interviews and shadowing opportunities would illuminate how the teacher

133

trainers strengthen the teaching candidate's self-efficacy. Comparing information from interviews of Montessori trainers would show if the thoughts, logic, and benefits stemming from their initiatives for self-efficacy promotion are similar, and what the ensuing impact is on students.

Replicating this study in different parts of the world would provide data from schools comprising different demographics. Not only would this supply comparative information and a larger area in which to generalize findings can be generalized, but it could also reconcile some of the cultural discrepancies noted earlier. Since Montessori schools exist all over the world with the same educational materials, studies of this nature are feasible.

In addition, it would be beneficial to study self-efficacy in pre-service and in-service teachers and observe the relationship with observed levels of self-efficacy and student achievement. Previous studies (Walker, 1992) have shown student achievement and self-efficacy to be related. It would also be interesting to take this research into the public school setting, where Montessori schools are now becoming popular, and assessing levels of efficacy of pre-service teachers after some experience in the public sector.

Finally, developing techniques for measuring teacher self-efficacy in the first place would really contribute to the field. While studies have shown the TSES to be valid and reliable for measuring overall teacher efficacy, it may not be fully suited for measuring Montessori teacher self-efficacy. Besides the TSES survey, a Perceptions in

Participation (PIP) questionnaire was prepared to examine which of the influences predicted self-efficacy most accurately. As far as the intricacies of this particular study itself, the survey questions could—and have been—improved. Using SPSS, factor analysis was conducted to determine how closely the items fit into the constructs they were designed to assess. Several items were dropped because they did not fit well with the others. This survey instrument has since been changed and is presented in Appendix F; hopefully, other teacher-training organizations will use it and find it beneficial.

The 19 questions on the interview were mostly open-ended and gave the teacher trainees many opportunities to share their experiences. The one lapse was that the general questions were lacking, and I would request more specific examples in the future. This would apply, for example, to: "(3) Tell me about how you feel as a beginning Montessori teacher about to lead a class of children all by yourself." I would include questions like "Do you feel you can manage the classroom? What makes you think so?" or "Can you give me an example of a time when you handled a very difficult child in your classroom. How did you handle it?" On the whole though, the questionnaire was very effective and I did not witness the teacher trainees feeling uncomfortable at any point of their interview.

Conclusion

Teacher self-efficacy is a crucial factor in improving teacher education and promoting education reform as high teacher self-efficacy consistently correlates to positive student and teacher behaviors."What people think, believe, and feel affects how they behave. The natural and extrinsic effects of their actions, in turn, partly determine

135

their thought patterns and affective reactions" (Bandura, 1986, p. 25). As studies show, teachers' personal beliefs regarding their ability to affect student achievement account for some of the variance in teacher effectiveness (Armor, et al., 1976; Berman & McLaughlin, 1977). Hence, it is almost critical that teachers possess a strong self-efficacy that allows them to help children reach their full potential. It is possible that some teachers will acquire strong self-efficacy during their teacher training, while others will do so only after running their own classrooms.

As this study shows, students that experience success make for more confident teachers. It is therefore important for professional development programs and teacher-training institutions to provide their students with opportunities to experience success, and to make them feel supported. Each of the teachers I interviewed for this research study were very appreciative of their tutor and mentor, and spoke fondly of the relationships they formed with them.

Teacher educators need to consider all the sources of information that influence prospective teacher efficacy beliefs to enhance these during the training itself .if prospective teacher efficacy is to be enhanced during teacher education programs. Teachers— Montessori and others must be provided with opportunities to experience success and to know they are supported. This will not only help those that have with a high sense of self-efficacy, but will also help and guide those that need to strengthen their self-efficacy. Only then will we be able to fulfill Maria Montessori's aim of an efficacious education, which "tends to help toward the complete unfolding of life. To be

136

thus helpful it is necessary rigorously to avoid the arrest of spontaneous movements and the imposition of arbitrary tasks" (1912, p. 88). The hope of educational reform lies in the transforming individual attitudes, is that the adult is no longer an impediment to the child's inherently natural development.

APPENDICES

APPENDIX A

LETTER TO SCHOOLS REQUESTING PARTICIPATION IN RESEARCH STUDY.

June 7th, 2011

Dear Director,

My name is Punum Bhatia and I am the Director of Montessori Casa International (MACTE accredited) in Denver, CO. I am also a PhD student at the University of Colorado Denver. As a part of my dissertation I am conducting research to gain a better understanding of the influences on self-efficacy for Montessori teachers. Teaching efficacy is an individual's perceived level of effectiveness for completing a teaching task. Clearly, an investigation into pre service teacher self-efficacy and how these beliefs are conceived and nurtured can provide meaningful information to teacher educators and professionals responsible for designing and implementing more meaningful teacher preparation programs.

The research will be conducted in two parts. The first part is just before the students embark on their Montessori training. They will be asked to take a simple survey consisting of 24 questions that they answer on Survey Monkey. This will indicate their level of self-efficacy. Then in December they will be asked to take the same survey again as well as another one consisting of 12 questions. This is also on Survey Monkey and will indicate the influences on their level of self-efficacy. Participants will be ranked by growth and the top 3 and bottom 3 will be interviewed. The interview will be a semi-structured design and will be conducted over the phone.

I appreciate your help and support in conducting this important research that will help us meet the needs of our students and improve the quality of our training. I am attaching the letter as well as the link to the survey for you to forward to your students. Please copy me on that email so I will be able to follow up with them.

Please contact me via phone (303.523.7590) or email (pb@mcidenver.edu) if you have questions or concerns.

Thank you so much.

Punum Bhatia

Director

I give permission to Punum Bhatia to recruit our students for the purpose of this research.

_____   _____

Name   and signature   Date

APPENDIX B

CONSENT APPROVAL FORM

Date: June 2, 2011   Valid for Use

Through:

Study Title: An Investigation into Sources of Montessori Teacher Self-Efficacy

Principal Investigator: Punum Bhatia

COMIRB No: 11-0317

Version Date: June 2, 2011

Version #: 1

You are being asked to be in a research study conducted by Punum Bhatia. Punum is a doctoral student at the University of Colorado Denver. She can be reached at 303.523.7590. This form provides you with information about the study. Please read the information below and ask questions about anything you don't understand before deciding whether or not to take part.

Why is this study being done?

This study plans to learn more about the influences on Montessori teacher self-efficacy. A teacher's sense of efficacy has been consistently recognized as an important attribute of effective teaching and has been positively correlated to teacher and student outcomes. You are being asked to be in this research study because you are training to become a Montessori teacher. Participation in this study is entirely your choice.

Other people in this study

For this study, there is neither an experimental nor a control group. The research is simply exploring various levels of Montessori teacher self-efficacy and the possible influences on the different levels. The study will be conducted in two parts. The initial study will consist of asking 100 participants around the country to complete a questionnaire instrument measuring teacher self-efficacy and other possible influences on self-efficacy. This will be conducted at the beginning of the training program. A similar questionnaire will be conducted during the internship period of the training. The next part of the study will involve selecting 6 participants for an interview to more fully explore the influences identified in the questionnaire analysis.

What happens if I join this study?

If you join the study, you will be asked to complete a questionnaire that consists of 24 questions once in the beginning of your teacher training program and once when you near completion. As part of this study, you may be asked to participate in a one hour interview that will explore more deeply the influences on Montessori teacher self-efficacy. The interview will be conducted by Punum Bhatia at the location of your choice. The questions will be related to the questionnaire results from the initial phase of the research study. The interview will be audio taped in order to ensure accuracy of the information provided. You may request a copy of the audiotape and the taping will be stopped at any part of the interview at your request.

What are the possible discomforts or risks?

There are no foreseeable risks to participating in this research. At any time, if the questions cause the participant any discomfort, the participant can elect to stop the interview or skip the question. There is a slight risk of breach of confidentiality, thus in order to minimize this risk, access to the audiotapes and transcripts of the interviews will be limited to the principal investigator and her advisor.

What are the possible benefits of the study?

This study is designed for the researcher to learn more about Montessori teacher self-efficacy. By participating in this study, you will have the opportunity to learn more about your individual self-efficacy and your participation will benefit the teaching community by providing more valuable information of Montessori teacher self-efficacy influences.

Will I be paid for being in the study?

You will not be paid to be in the study.

Will I have to pay for anything?

It will not cost you anything to be in the study.

Is my participation voluntary?

Taking part in this study is voluntary. You have the right to choose not to take part in this study. If you choose to take part, you have the right to stop at any time. If you refuse or decide to withdraw later, you will not lose any benefits or rights to which you are entitled.

Who do I call if I have questions?

The researcher carrying out this study is Punum Bhatia. You may ask any questions you have now. If you have questions, concerns, or complaints later, you may call Punum at 303.523.7590. You will be given a copy of this form to keep.

You may have questions about your rights as someone in this study. You can call Punum with questions. You can also call the Colorado Multiple Institutional Review Board (COMIRB). You can call them at 303-724-1055.

Who will see my research information?

We will do everything we can to keep your records a secret. It cannot be guaranteed.

Both the records that identify you and the consent form signed by you may be looked at by others. They are:

- Federal agencies that monitor human subject research
- The Colorado Multiple Institutional Review Board (COMIRB)
- The group doing the study
- People at the Colorado Multiple Institutional Review Board (COMIRB) who want to make sure the research is safe

We might talk about this research study at meetings. We might also print the results of this research study in relevant journals. But we will always keep the names of the research subjects, like you, private.

Agreement to be in this study

I have read this paper about the study or it was read to me. I understand the possible risks and benefits of this study. I know that being in this study is voluntary. I choose to be in this study: I will get a copy of this consent form.

Signature:_____ Date:_____

Print Name:_____

Investigator:_____ Date:_____

APPENDIX C

LETTER WITH SURVEY TO STUDENTS

Research Survey on Montessori Teacher Self-Efficacy

My name is Punum Bhatia and I am a PhD student at the University of Colorado Denver. This survey is designed to provide information for my dissertation research study. I would like to thank you for taking the time to complete this survey. Participation is voluntary. Your answers will help me to investigate the influences on Montessori teacher self-efficacy. Teaching efficacy is an individual's perceived level of effectiveness for completing a teaching task. The results of this study will only be used to help inform teacher education and professional development programs and participation will also give you the opportunity to learn more about your individual teacher self-efficacy. You may contact me at any time in order to request your individual results and the combined results of this survey. The risks of this study are minimal and may include discomfort, potential loss of confidentiality, etc. You may discontinue the survey at any time. All responses will be kept entirely confidential. Your name will be removed from the survey and you will be referred to at all times by a coded number. I will be the only person with access to these records. The completed survey instruments will be securely stored for three years and then destroyed. I will do everything I can to keep your records confidential but this cannot, however, be guaranteed. If you have any questions or concerns during or after your participation, please contact me at 303.523.7590 or pb@mcidenver.edu.. You may also contact the Colorado Multiple Institution Review Board at 303.724.1055 or via email at comirb@ucdenver.edu.

147

Please follow the link http://www.surveymonkey.com/s/XZLZ368 and answer the following questions as truthfully as possible. Thank you again for participating in this important work.

APPENDIX D

TEACHER SENSE OF EFFICACY SCALE

Teacher Sense of Efficacy Scale (TSES)

A. This questionnaire is designed to help us gain a better understanding of the kinds of things that create challenges for teachers. Your answers are confidential.

Directions: Please indicate your opinion about each of the questions below by marking any one of the nine responses in the columns, ranging from (1) "None at all" to (9) "A Great Deal" as each represents a degree on the continuum. Please respond to each of the questions by considering the combination of your current ability, resources, and opportunity to do each of the following in your present position.

1. How much can you do to get through to the most difficult students?

2. How much can you do to help your students think critically?

3. How much can you do to motivate students who show low interest in school work?

4. To what extent can you make your expectations clear about student behavior?

5. How much can you do to get students to believe they can do well in school work?

6. How well can you respond to difficult questions from your students?

7. How much can you do to control disruptive behavior in the classroom

8. How well can you establish routines to keep activities running smoothly?

9. How much can you do to help your students value learning?

10. How much can you gauge student comprehension of what you have taught?

11. To what extent can you craft good questions for your students?

12. How much can you do to foster student creativity?

13. How much can you do to get children to follow classroom rules?

14. How much can you do to improve the understanding of a student who is failing?

15. How much can you do to calm a student who is disruptive or noisy?

16. How well can you establish a classroom management system with each group of students?

17. How much can you do to adjust your lessons to the proper level for individual students?

18. How much can you use a variety of assessment strategies?

19. How well can you keep a few problem students from running an entire lesson?

20. To what extent can you provide an alternative explanation or example when students are confused?

21. How well can you respond to defiant students?

22. How much can you assist families in helping their children do well in school?

23. How well can you implement alternative strategies in your classroom?

24. How well can you provide appropriate challenges for very capable students?

APPENDIX E

PERCEPTIONS IN PARTICIPATION 1

Perceptions in Participation I

These questions are designed to help us gain a better understanding of the influences on a Montessori teacher's self-efficacy. Please indicate your opinion about each of the statements by circling only one number that best represents your opinion.

1. In my early experience of working with young children I generally felt successful.

2. I can recall experiences I have had working with difficult, unmotivated children, in which I successfully engaged them in productive activity.

3. Rate your satisfaction with your professional performance this year on a scale of 1 to 5 (5=Very Good).

4. I have had experiences presenting Montessori materials to children that have built my confidence as a teacher.

5. I felt that my advisor/mentor was supportive during my internship and this helped my confidence.

6. In my preparation I was able to observe truly skilled teachers..

7. My advisor/mentor played a positive role in my development as a teacher.

8. Rate the interpersonal support provided by colleagues at your school this year on a scale of 1 to 5 (5+Very Good).

9. People I respect have told me I will be a good teacher.

10. I have people I can rely on who express confidence in me as a teacher.

11. My instructors encouraged me in ways that built my confidence.

153

12. My advisor/mentor provided me with positive, constructive feedback which was very useful to me.

13. In the work I have done with children, I have had a feeling of well being.

14. I have been nervous and experienced physical symptoms of anxiety while working with children.

15. I try to talk and explain my stress in order to get feedback from my colleagues.

16. At times when a child is being disruptive and not listening to me, I experienced sweaty palms or increased heart beat.

APPENDIX F

PERCEPTIONS IN PARTICIPATION II

Perceptions in Participation II

These questions are designed to help us gain a better understanding of the influences on a Montessori teacher's self-efficacy. Please indicate your opinion about each of the statements by circling only one number that best represents your opinion.

1. I do not hesitate to return to a lesson that has not worked well in the past.
2. While working with difficult students, I managed to successfully engage them in productive activity.
3. This school year my successes outweigh my failures.
4. There are certain Montessori materials I fall back on to rebound from setbacks.
5. My advisor/mentor guided me during my internship and I rely on his/her methods in my own teaching.
6. In my teacher training I observed adept teachers.
7. I often reflect on how my advisor/mentor would handle a situation and react similarly.
8. Rate the support provided by school colleagues on a scale from 1 to 5.
9. My advisor/mentor provided me with positive feedback that supported by career choice.
10. My friends and family often praise my work as a teacher.
11. My instructors build my confidence by encouraging my teaching skills.
12. I usually take into consideration my advisor/mentor's advice.
13. When I am distracted or tense my students sense those feelings.

14. If preoccupied with personal matters I am unable to concentrate on the lesson at hand.

15. I discuss my challenges with my colleagues to manage my stress.

16. At times when a child is being disruptive and not listening to me, I experienced sweaty palms or increased heart beat.

APPENDIX F

INTERVIEW PROTOCOL

Interview Protocol

Introduction

You have been selected to speak with us today because you have been identified as someone who has a great deal to share about learning and teaching. I am interested in exploring the influences on Montessori teacher self-efficacy levels and how people feel about themselves as teachers. We will be exploring your personal experiences with learning and then moving on to more teaching related influences.

To facilitate note-taking, I would like to audio tape our conversations today. Only researchers on the project will be privy to the tapes that will be eventually destroyed after they are transcribed. Human subject requires that you sign a special form that protects your rights. Essentially, this document states that: (1) all information will be held confidential, (2) your participation is voluntary and you may stop at any time if you feel uncomfortable, and (3) we do not intend to inflict any harm. But it is possible that the process of answering the questions could lead you to feel uncomfortable or embarrassed. Thank you for agreeing to participate.

We have planned this interview to last no longer than one hour. During this time, I have several questions that we would like to cover. If time begins to run short, it may be necessary to interrupt you in order to push ahead and complete this line of questioning.

Personal Learning Experiences

1. Tell me about your Montessori training and elements of the course you enjoyed most.

   Probe: In what ways did the course impact you? Positively or negatively?

2. Just as there are parts of training that students enjoy, there are often things that students wish were different in their training. What, if anything, do you wish were different.

3. Tell me about how you feel as a beginning Montessori teacher about to lead a class of children all by yourself.

4. In which areas has your confidence as a Montessori teacher increased because of your training? In what areas has it decreased?

5. What aspects of the training most impacted your confidence as a teacher?

6. Tell me about some of your successes and failures as a student as a student in high school.

7. How would you describe yourself as a future teacher.

8. How confident do you feel to successfully teach all the curriculum areas even to the most difficult students?

Teaching Efficacy – Influences

9. What or who would you say influenced you to become a Montessori teacher?

10. Tell me about what you have read that influenced your teaching.

11. Who would you say influenced you positively during your training? Negatively?

12. Could you rank in order of importance what influence was the most important to you in the training:

- Lectures

- Demonstrations

- Peer support

- Teacher

- Practice teaching

- Mentor

13. Tell me about your advisor/mentor relationship. How often did you meet?

    Probe: Do you think your mentor/advisor had an impact on your confidence as a teacher? How? What were the advantages and disadvantages of this mentor experience? Will you keep in contact with your mentor?

14. Do you share your achievements on Facebook or Twitter/

15. Sometimes families and friends of students are supportive and sometimes they are not. How supportive are your family and friends of you being a Montessori teacher?

16. What provides you with motivation and inspiration?

17. What are the causes of your stress and anxiety?

    Probe: How do you deal with it?

18. Could you tell me one story about when you felt least successful as a Montessori teacher?

19. Could you tell me one story about when you felt most successful as a Montessori teacher.

BIBLIOGRAPHY

Armor, D., Conroy-Oseguera, P., Cox, M., King, N., McDonnell, L., Pascal, A., Pauly, E., & Zellman, G. (1979). *Analysis of the school preferred reading programs in selected Los Angeles minority schools, REPORT NO. R-2007-LAUSD*. Santa Monica, CA: Rand Corporation.

Allinder, R.M. (1994). The relationship between efficacy and instructional practices of special education teachers and consultants. *Teacher Education and Special Education*.17:86–95.

Ashton, P., Olejnik, S., Crocker, L., & McAuliffe, M. (1982*). Measurement problems in the study of teachers' sense of efficacy*. Paper presented at the annual meeting of the American Educational Research Association, New York.

Ashton, P. T., Webb, R. B., & Doda, N. (1983). A study of teachers' sense of efficacy. National Institute of Education.

Ashton, P. T., & Webb, R. B. (1986). *Making a difference: Teachers' sense of efficacy and student achievement*. New York: Longman.

Bandura, A., (1977). Self-efficacy: Toward a unifying theory of behavioral change. *Psychological Review*, 84 (2), 191-215.

Bandura, A. (1982). Self-efficacy mechanisms in human agency. *American Psychologist*. Vol 37, pp 122 – 147.

Bandura, A. (1986). Social foundations of thought and action: A social cognitive theory. Englewood Cliffs, New Jersey: Prentice Hall.

Bandura, A. (1993). Perceived self-efficacy in cognitive development and functioning. *Educational Psychologist, 28*(2), 117–148.

Bandura, A. (1995). *Self-efficacy in changing societies.* Cambridge, U.K.: Cambridge University Press.

Bandura, A. (1997). *Self-efficacy: The exercise of control.* New York: W. H. Freeman.

Bandura, A. (2001). Social cognitive theory: An agentic perspective. *Annual Review of Psychology, 52*, 1-26.

Bandura, A. (2006). "Toward a Psychology of Human Agency". *Perspectives on Psychological Science* 1: 2.

Bandura, A. (2007). Much ado over a faulty conception of perceived self-efficacy grounded in faulty experimentation. *Journal of Social and Clinical Psychology, 26*(6), 641-658.

Bennett, J. G., et al. (1984). *The Spiritual Hunger of the Modern Child.* Charles Town, W.V: Claymont Communications.

Berg, B.L. (2004). *Qualitative research methods for the social sciences* (5th ed.). Boston: Pearson Education, Inc.

Berman, P., & McLaughlin, M.W. (1977). *Federal programs supporting educational change*. Vol VII: Factors affecting implementation and continuation (Report No. R-1589/7 HEW). Santa Monica, CA. : The RAND Corporation.

Billingsley, B.S., Cross L.H. (1992). Predictors of commitment, job satisfaction, and intent to stay in teaching: A comparison of general and special educators. *The Journal of Special Education,* 25,453–471.

Billingsley B, Carlson E, Klein S. (2004). The working conditions and induction support of early career special educators. *Exceptional Children*, 70,333-347.

Bodrova, E. (2003). Vygotsky and Montessori: One dream, two visions. *Montessori Life*, 15 91), 30-33.

Boe, E.E., Barkanic G., Leow C.S. (1999). Retention and attrition of teachers at the school level: National trends and predictors. Philadelphia, PA: University of Pennsylvania, Graduate School of Education, Center for Research and Evaluation in Social Policy. (ERIC Document reproduction Service No. ED436485)

Borko, H., & Putnam, R. T. (1996). Learning to teach. In Berliner, D. & Calfee, R. (Eds.) *Handbook of Educational Psychology*. New York: Macmillan.

Boyer L, Gillespie P.(2000). Keeping the committed. *Teaching Exceptional Children*.33:10–15.

164

Brookover, W., Schweitzer, J., Schneider, J., Beady, C., Flood, P., & Wisenbaker, J. (1978). Elementary school climate and school achievement. *American Educational Research Journal,* 15, 301 – 318.

Brophy, J. E., & Everston, C. (1977). Teacher behaviors and student learning in second and third grades. In G. D. Borich (Ed.), *The appraisal of teaching: Concepts and process* (pp. 79 – 95). Reading, MA: Addison-Wesley.

Cantrell, P. (2003). Traditional vs. retrospective pretests for measuring science teaching efficacy beliefs in preservice teachers. *School Science & Mathematics, 103*(4), 177-185.

Cantrell, P., Young, S. & Moore, A. (2003). Factors affecting science teaching efficacy of pre- service elementary teachers. *Journal of Science Teacher Education. 61,* 433-445.

Chattin-McNichols,J. (1992). *The Montessori Controversy.* New York: Delmar Publication.

Charalambous, C. Y., Philippou, G. N., & Kyriakides, L. (2008). Tracing the development of preservice teachers' efficacy beliefs in teaching mathematics during fieldwork. *Education   Study Mathematics*, 67, 125-142.

Charmaz, K. (2006). *Constructing grounded theory: A practical guide through qualitative analysis.* Thousand Oaks, C.A: Sage Publications.

Chester, M. D., & Beaudin, B. Q. (1996). Efficacy beliefs of newly hired teachers in urban schools. *American Educational Research Journal, 33*(1), 233-257.

Chwalitsz, K., Altameyer, E.M., Russel, D.W.91992). Causal attributions, self-efficacy, cognitions, and coping with stress. Journal of Social and Clinical Research.11:377–400.

Corry, S.K. (2006). *A comparison of Montessori students to general education students as they move from middle school into a traditional high school program.* University of Nebraska.

Creswell, J. W. (1998). *Qualitative inquiry and research design: Choosing among the five traditions.* Thousand Oaks, CA: Sage.

Creswell, J. W., & Plano Clark, V. L. (2007). *Designing and conducting mixed methods research.* Thousand Oaks, CA: Sage.

Cohen, J. (1988). *Statistical power analysis for the behavioral sciences.* Routledge Academic

Collins, K. M. T., Onwuegbuzie, A. J., & Sutton, I. L. (2006). A model incorporating the rationale and purpose for conducting mixed-methods research in special education and beyond. *Learning Disabilities: A Contemporary Journal, 4*(1), 67-100.

Conger, J. C., & Keane, S. P. (1981). Social skills intervention in the treatment of isolated or withdrawn children. *Psychological Bulletin, 90,* 478-495.

Czernaik, C. M. (1990). *A study of self-efficacy, anxiety, and science knowledge in pre-service elementary teachers*. Paper presented at the National Association for Research in Science Teaching, Atlanta, GA.

Darling-Hammond L. & McLaughlin M.W. (1995). Policies that support professional development in an era of reform. *Phi Delta Kappan, 76* (8), 597 – 604.

Dembo, M.H. & Gibson, S. (1985). Teachers' sense of efficacy: An important factor in school improvement. *The Elementary School Journal.* 86 (2), 173 – 184.

Denzine, G. M., Cooney, J. B., & McKenzie, R. (2005). Confimatory factor analysis of the Teacher Efficacy Scale for prospective teachers. *British Journal of Educational Psychology, 75*, 689-708.

Denzin, N.K., & Lincoln, Y.S. (2005). Introduction: The discipline and practice of qualitative research. In N.K. Denzin & Y.S. Lincoln (Eds). *The sage handbook of qualitative research* (Chapter 1: pp. 1-32). Thousand Oaks: SAGE Publications.

Eaton, M.J., & Dembo, M.H. (1997). Differences in the motivation beliefs of Asian American and non-Asian students. *Journal of Educational Psychology*, 89, 443-440.

Elkind, D. (1974). Montessori and Piaget. In *Children and Adolescents: Interpretive essays on Jean Piaget* (Second edition). New York: Oxford University Press, 128-138.

167

Elkind, D. (2003). Montessori and constructivism. *Montessori Life*, 15 (1): 26-29.

Emmer, E. T., & Hickman, J. (1991). Teacher efficacy in classroom management and discipline. *Educational and Psychological Measurement, 51*(3), 755-765.

Enochs, L. G., & Riggs, I. M. (1990). *Further development of an elementary science teaching efficacy belief instrument: A preservice elementary scale.* Paper presented at the Annual Meeting of the National Association for Research in Science Teaching.

Enochs, L. G., Smith, P. L., & Huinker, D. (2000). Establishing factor validity of the mathematics teaching efficacy beliefs instrument. *School Science & Mathematics, 100*, 194-202.

Fang, Z.. & Ashley, C. (2004). Preservice teachers' interpretations of a field-based reading block. *Journal of Teacher Education, 55*(1), 39-54.

Fives, H., Hamman, D., & Olivarez, A. (2007). Does burnout begin with student-teaching? Analyzing efficacy, burnout, and support during the student-teaching semester. *Teaching and Teacher Education, 23*, 916-934.

Fortman, C. K., & Pontius, R. (2000). *Self-efficacy during student teaching.* Paper presented at the Annual Meeting of the Mid-Western Educational Research Association.

Friedman, I. A., & Kass, E. (2002). Teacher self-efficacy: a classroom-organization conceptualization. *Teaching and Teacher Education, 18*, 675-686.

Gaskill, P.J., Woolfolk Hoy, A.(2002). Self-efficacy and self-regulated learning: The dynamic duo in school performance. In: Aronson J, editor. *Improving academic achievement: Impact of psychological factors on education.* San Diego, CA: Academic Press. pp.185–208.

Gay, L. R. & Airasian, P. (2000). Educational research competencies for analysis and application (6th ed.). Englewood Cliffs, NJ: Prentice-Hall.

Gibson, S., & Dembo, M. H. (1984). Teacher efficacy: A construct validation. *Journal of Educational Psychology*, 76(4), 503–511.

Goodwin, W.L., & Goodwin, L. D. (1996). *Understanding quantitative and qualitative research in early childhood education.* New York, NY: Teacher College Press.

Guskey, T. R. (1984). The influence of change in instructional effectiveness upon the affective characteristics of teachers. *American Educational Research Journal 21* (2), 245 – 259.

Guskey, T. R. (1987). Context variables that affect measures of teacher efficacy. *Journal of Educational research*, 81 (1), 41 – 47.

Guskey, T. (1988). Teacher efficacy, self-concept, and attitudes toward the
    implementation of instructional innovation. *Teaching and Teacher Education,*
    4(1), 63–69.

Hainstock, E.G. (1997). *The essential Montessori: An introduction to the woman, the*
    writings, the method, and the movement. New York: Plume.

Haverback, H.R., & Parault, S. J. (2008). Pre-service reading teacher efficacy and
    tutoring: A review. *Educational Psychology Review, 20,* 237-255.

Heneman, H. G., III, Kimball, S., & Milanowski, A. (2006). The teacher sense of efficacy
    scale: Validation evidence and behavioral prediction [Electronic Version].
    University of Wisconsin-Madison, Wisconsin Center for Education Research.
    Retrieved July 25, 2012.

Henson, R. K. (2002). From adolescent angst to adulthood: Substantive implications and
    measurement dilemmas in the development of teacher self-efficacy research.
    Educational Psychologist, 37, 137-150.

Hollon, S. D., & Beck, A. T. (1994). Cognitive and cognitive-behavioral therapies. In A.
    E. Bergin & S. L. Garfield (Eds.), Handbook of psychotherapy and behavior
    change (4^(th) Ed.) (pp. 428-466). New York: Wiley.

Hoy, W. & Woolfolk, A. (1990, Summer). Socialization of student teachers. *American*
    Educational Research Journal, 27 (92), 279 – 300.

Hoy,W. & Woolfolk, A. (1993). Teachers' sense of efficacy and the organizational health of schools. *Elementary School Journal*, 93 (4), 355 – 372.

James, W. (1890). *The principles of psychology*. New York: Dover Publications.

Jung, C.G. (1940). *The Integration of the Personality*. London: Routledge and Kegan Paul, Ltd.

Labone, E. (2004). Teacher efficacy: Maturing the construct through research in alternative paradigms. *Teaching and Teacher Education, 20*, 341-359.

Linek, W.M., Nelson, O.G., Sampson. M.B., Zeek, C.K., Mohr, K.A.J., & Hughes, L. (1999). Developing beliefs about literacy instruction: A cross-case analysis of preservice teachers in traditional and field-based settings. *Reading Research and Instruction, 38*, 371-386.

Leech, N. L., & Onwuegbuzie, A. J. (2007). A typology of mixed methods research designs. *Quality and Quantity: International Journal of Methodology*.

Katz, L. G. (1993). *Dispositions: Definitions and implications for early childhood practices*. Urbana, IL: ERIC Clearinghouse on Elementary and Early Childhood Education.

Kearns, D.T. (1988). *Winning the brain race: Bold plan to make our schools competitive.* ICS Press

Kegan, R. & Lahey, L.L. (2001). *How the way we talk can change the way we work: Seven languages for transformation.* San Francisco: Jossey-Bass.

Klassen, R.M. (2004). Optimism and realism: A review of self-efficacy from a cross-cultural perspective. *International Journal of Psychology*, 39, 205 – 230.

Kramer, R. (1976). *Maria Montessori: A biography.* New York: Putnam.

Labone, E.(2004). Teacher efficacy: Maturing the construct through research in alternative paradigms. *Teaching and Teacher Education.* 20:341–359.

LaPelle, N.R. (2004). Simplifying qualitative data analysis using general purpose software tools. *Preventive and Behavioral Medicine Publications and Presentations.* 84

Leech, N. L., & Onwuegbuzie, A. J. A typology of mixed methods research designs. *Quality and Quantity: International Journal of Methodology.*

Lillard, A. S. (2005). *Montessori: The science behind the genius.* New York: Oxford University Press.

Lillard, P.P. (1972). *Montessori: A modern approach.* New York: Schocken

McDermott, J.J. (1962). Introduction. In E.M. Standing (1962), *Maria Montessori: Her life and work.* New York: New American Library, xi –xv.

McLaughlin, M. & Berman, P. (1977). Retooling staff development in a period of retrenchment. *Educational Leadership. 35* (3), 191-194.

172

McLaughlin, M. W. & Marsh, D. (1978). Staff development and school change. *Teachers College Record*, 80 (1), 70-94.

Miles, M.B., and Huberman, A.M. (1994). *Qualitative data analysis: An expanded sourcebook. (2nd Edition).* Thousand Oaks, CA: SAGE Publications.

Minggang,W., & Yuan, C. (2004). A review of cross-cultural researchers on the relationship of thinking and language. *Psychological Science*, 27, 431 – 433.

Montessori, M. (1912/1964). *The Montessori method*. New York:Schocken.

Montessori, M. (1914/1965). *Dr. Montessori's own handbook.* New York: Schocken .

Montessori, M. (1916). The advanced Montessori method -- II. Oxford: Clio.

Montessori, M. (1917/1965). Spontaneous activity in education: The advanced Montessori   method. Oxford: Clio.

Montessori, M. (1946/1963). *Education for a new world*. Madras, India: Kalakshetra.

Montessori, M. (1948/1967). To educate the human potential. Madras, India: Kalakshetra.

Montessori, M. (1948/1976). From childhood to adolescence. New York: Schocken.

Montessori, M. (1949/1974). Childhood education. Chicago: Henry Regnery.

Montessori, M. (1966). *The secret of childhood*. New York: Ballantine Books.

Montessori, M. (1979). *The child society and the world*. Oxford: Clio.

Montessori, M. (1989). *The child in the family*. Oxford: Clio.

Montessori, M. (1949/1992). *Education and Peace*. Oxford: Clio.

Montessori, M. (1934/1997). *Basic ideas of Montessori's educational theory*. Oxford: Clio.

Montessori, M. (1948/1997). *The discovery of the child*. Oxford: Clio.

Montessori, M. (1949/2007). *The absorbent mind*. Oxford: Clio.

Morrison, G.M., Walker, D., Wakefield, P., Solberg, S. (1994). Teacher preferences for collaborative relationships: Relationship to efficacy for teaching in prevention-related domains. *Psychology in the Schools*.31:221–231.

Moore, W., & Esselman, M. (1992). Teacher efficacy, power, school climate and achievement: A desegregating district's experience. *Paper presented at the Annual Meeting of the American Educational Research Association,* San Francisco.

Mulholland, J. & Wallace, J. (2001). Teacher induction and elementary science teaching: Enhancing self-efficacy. *Teaching and Teacher Education, 17,* 243-261.

Oppenheimer, T. (1999). *Schooling the imagination*. Atlantic Monthly, 284(3), 71-83.

Pajares, F. (1992). Teachers' beliefs and educational research: Cleaning up a messy construct.*Review of Educational Research, 62*(3), 307-332.

Pajares, F. (1997). Current directions in self-efficacy research. In M. Maehr & P.R. Pintrich (Eds.). *Advances in motivation and achievement*, 10, 1 - 49.

Pajares, F. (2002). *Self-efficacy beliefs in academic contexts: An outline.* Retrieved July
30, 2012 from http:// www.emory.edu/EDUCATION/mfp/efftalk.html

Pajares,F. (2003). Self-efficacy beliefs, motivation, and achievement in writing: A review
of the literature. *Reading and Writing Quarterly*, 19 (2), 139-158.

Palmer, D. H. (2006). Durability of changes in self-efficacy of pre-service primary
teachers. *International Journal of Science Education, 28*(6), 655-671.

Philippou, G., & Charalambos, C. Y. (2005). *Disentangling mentors' role in the
development of prospective teachers' efficacy beliefs in teaching mathematics.*
Paper presented at the 28th Conference of the International Group for the
Psychology of Mathematics Education, Melbourne, Australia.

Pintrich, P. R., & Schunk, D.H. (1996). *Motivation in education: Theory, research, and
applications.* Englewood Cliffs, NJ: Merrill/Prentice Hall.

Postman, N. (1999). *Building a bridge to the eighteenth century: How the past can
improve our future.* Melbourne: Scribe Publications.

Poulou, M. (2007). Personal teaching efficacy and its sources: Student teachers'
perceptions. *Educational Psychology, 27*(2), 191-218.

Riggs, I. M., & Enochs, L. G. (1990). Toward the development of an elementary teacher's
science teaching efficacy belief instrument. *Science Education, 74*, 625-637.

Roberts, J. K., & Henson, R. K. (2001). *A confirmatory factor analysis of a new measure of teacher efficacy: Ohio state teacher efficacy scale.* Paper presented at the American Educational Research Association.

Rose, J.S. & Medway, F. J. (1981). Measurement of teachers' beliefs in their control over student outcome. *Journal of Educational Research 74* (3), 185-190.

Ross, J. A. (1992). Teacher efficacy and the effects of coaching on student achievement. *Canadian Journal of Education, 17*(1), 51-65.

Ross, J.A. (1998). The antecedents and consequences of teacher efficacy. In: Brophy J, editor. Advances in research on teaching. Greenwich, CT JAI Press. 7, 49-73.

Rotter, J. B. (1966). Generalized expectancies for internal versus external control of reinforcement. *Psychological Monographs, 80*, 1-28.

Ruenzel, D. (1997). The Montessori Method. *Teacher Magazine, 8* (7), 30 -35.

Rushton, S. P. (2000). Student teacher efficacy in inner-city schools. *The Urban Review, 32* (3), 365-383.

Rushton, S.P. (2003). Two preservice teachers' growth in self-efficacy while teaching in an inner-city school. *The Urban Review, 35* (3). 167-189.

Schapiro, D. (1993). What is Montessori education is part of the answer? *Education Digest, 58* (7), 40 – 43.

Scholz, U., Gutierrez-Dona, B., Sud,S., & Schwarzer, R. (2002). Is general self-efficacy a universal construct? Psychometric findings from 25 countries. *European journal of Psychological Assessment.* 18 (3), 242 – 251.

Schunk, D. H. (1988). *Perceived self-efficacy and related social cognitive processes as predictors of student academic performance.* Paper presented at the American Educational Research Association.

Schwarzer, R., Hallum, S. (2008). Perceived teacher self-efficacy as a predictor of job stress and burnout: Mediation analyses. *Applied Psychology: An International Review. 57*, 152-171.

Scribner, J.P. (1998). *Teacher efficacy and teacher professional learning: What school leaders should know.* Paper presented at the Annual Convention of the University Council for Educational Administration. St. Louis, MO.

Smylie, M.A. (1990). Teacher efficacy at work. In P. Reyes (Ed.), *Teachers and Their Workplace.* (pp. 48-66). Newbury Park: Sage.

Soodak, L. C., & Podell, D. M. (1996). Teacher efficacy: Toward the understanding of a multi-faceted construct. *Teaching and Teacher Education, 12*(4), 401-411.

Spradley, J. P. (1979). *The ethnographic interview.* Ft. Worth, FL: Harcourt Brace J

Standing, E.M. (1957). *Maria Montessori: Her life and work*. New York: Penguin.

Strauss, A., & Corbin, J. (1998). *Basics of qualitative research: Techniques and procedures for developing grounded theory (2nd ed.).* CA: Sage.

Tschannen-Moran, M., & Woolfolk Hoy, A. (2001). Teacher efficacy: Capturing an elusive construct. *Teaching and Teacher Education, 17*, 783-805.

Tschannen-Moran, M., & Woolfolk Hoy, A. (2007). The differential antecedents of self-efficacy beliefs of novice and experienced teachers. *Teaching and Teacher Education, 23*, 944– 956.

Tschannen-Moran, M., Woolfolk Hoy, A., & Hoy, W. K. (1998). Teacher efficacy: Its meaning and measure. *Review of Educational Research*, 68(2), 202–248.

Usher E.L., Pajares F. (2008). Sources of self-efficacy in school: Critical review of the literature and future directions. *Review of Educational Research*, 78,751-796.

Volkman, B. K., Scheffler, A. J., & Dana, M. E. (1992). *Enhancing preservice teachers' self-efficacy through a field-based program of reflective practice.* Paper presented at the Annual Meeting of the Mid-South Educational Research Association.

Walker, L. (1992). *Perceptions of preservice teacher efficacy.* Paper presented at the Annual Meeting of the Mid-South Educational Research Association. Knoxville, TN.

Ware, H., Kitsantas, A. (2007). Teacher and collective efficacy beliefs as predictors of professional commitment. *Journal of Educational Research. 100*, 303-310.

Watson, S. (1991). *A study of the effects of teacher efficacy on the academic achievement of third-grade students in selected elementary schools in South Carolina.* Unpublished doctoral dissertation, South Carolina State College, Orangebury. (University Microfilms No. UMI 9230552).

Watters, J. J., Ginns, I.S. (2000). Developing motivation to teach elementary science: Effect of collaborative and authentic learning practices in pre-service education. *Journal of Science Teacher Education.* 11, 301-321.

Wolf, Aline D. (1996). *Nurturing the spirit.* Parent Child Press PA

Woolfolk, A.E., Rosoff, B., Hoy, W.K. (1990). Teachers' sense of efficacy and their beliefs about managing students. *Teaching and Teacher Education.*6:137–148.

Woolfolk Hoy, A. (2000). *Changes in teacher efficacy during the early years of teaching.* Paper presented at the Annual Meeting of the American Educational Research Association, New Orleans, LA.

Woolfolk Hoy, A. (2001). Leading for learning: An educational psychologist's perspective. *UCEA: The Review*, 43 (3), 1-4.

Woolfolk Hoy, A. (2004). The educational psychology of teacher efficacy. *Educational Psychology Review*, 16, 153-176.

Woolfolk Hoy, A., & Burke-Spero, R. (2005). Changes in teacher efficacy during the early years of teaching: A comparison of four measures. *Teaching and Teacher Education, 21*(4), 343-356.

Worth, J., & Patterson, E. (2001). I can't wait to see Carlos!: Preservice teachers, situated learning, and personal relationships with students. *Journal of Literacy Research, 33*, 303-344.

Made in the USA
Lexington, KY
28 February 2015